To Deway
I pray this book will inspire you to live your best life. God Bless!

12/13/23

To Dewayne
I pray this book will
inspire you to live your
best life. God Bless!

12/13/'22

Playing The Trump Card

Using Faith to Succeed in Two Americas

Eric Moore

Scriptures noted NKJV are taken from the New King James Version. Copyright 1979, 1980, 1982, Thomas Nelson, Inc., Publishers.

Excerpts of speeches reprinted by arrangement with The Heirs to the Estate of Martin Luther King Jr., c/o Writers House as agent for the proprietor New York, NY. 1. Copyright © 1967 Dr. Martin Luther King, Jr. © renewed 1995 Coretta Scott King. 2. Copyright © 1968 Dr. Martin Luther King, Jr. © renewed 1996 Coretta Scott King.

Copyright © 2018 Eric Moore

All rights reserved.

ISBN:-13: 978-1973808084

ISBN-10:-1973808080

This book is dedicated to the memory of Trayvon Martin. I have had the pleasure of meeting his parents and I will honor them and his memory by continuing my efforts to make this world a better place. His name will never be forgotten. This book is also dedicated to my mentors Robert Allen, Patricia Hunter and Leo Moszczenski who each passed away during the writing process of this book.

ACKNOWLEDGMENTS

I would like to thank the following individuals who have helped sow seeds of encouragement into my life during the writing process of this book. Each of you challenges me to be the best man that I can be. I am grateful for your support and your prayers. I love each of you.

To my mother Marva, you have always been there for me encouraging me and believing in my abilities. You are simply the best. To my grandmother Mary, and the rest of my immediate and extended family, I thank each of you for your support and unwavering love during my lifetime. To Jennifa, you are a phenomenal woman and I thank you for inspiring me. To my godchildren and their parents, I thank you for always believing in me. To the men and women who have taken the time out of their lives to mentor me, I thank each of you for sowing your seeds of wisdom into my life. Special thanks to Jewell and Uleda Slayden, James Morton, Pastor Andre Williams, Pastor Thomas Robinson, Bishop Kevin Adams, Darryl Holloway, Vanessa Cottman, Stacey Wallace, and my Windward family. To my readers, I am able to live my dreams because of you. I thank each of you for your support.

Contents

Part One   **Out of Egypt**

Chapter 1	Making America Great	02
Chapter 2	Awakening From The Dream	12
Chapter 3	Where is our Joshua?	21
Chapter 4	The Price of Freedom	31
Chapter 5	Our Image and Our History	46
Chapter 6	Individualism vs Collectivism	60

Part Two   **Through The Wilderness**

Chapter 7	Survival to Success	71
Chapter 8	Playing The Trump Card	87
Chapter 9	Applied Faith	96
Chapter 10	Belief, Sight and Achievement	105
Chapter 11	From Belief to Blessing	113
Chapter 12	Remember Your Why	121
Chapter 13	The Power of The Anointing	131
Chapter 14	The Great I AM	139

Part Three   **The Promised Land**

Chapter 15	Promised Land Faith	150

Conclusion   164

PART ONE

OUT OF EGYPT

Chapter 1

Making America Great

The year 2019 will mark exactly four hundred years since the first group of enslaved Africans arrived in Jamestown, Virginia. Their arrival set the stage for what would become the epic exploitation of the unpaid slave labor of their descendants. The chattel slavery that began in 1619, created an imbalance in terms of economic and political power that has yet to be rectified in the United States of America. Slavery created a bicultural American caste system in this country that unjustly placed the descendants of enslaved Africans at the bottom of the social hierarchy and the descendants of European settlers at the top of the social hierarchy.

In the annals of history, there is another group of people who were dealt a similar unjust hand from the deck of destiny. They are known as the Israelites. Similarly, to the Africans in America, the Israelites were enslaved and exploited in an epic manner in the land of Egypt. In the book of Genesis there is an often overlooked passage of scripture that illustrates God's covenant with Abraham concerning his descendants. God said to him, "Know certainly that your descendants will be strangers in a land that is not theirs, and will serve them, and they will afflict them four hundred years. And also the nation whom they serve I will judge; afterward they shall come out with great possessions" (Genesis 13: 14-15).

God was true to His word to Abraham, and after nearly four hundred years of slavery and maltreatment, He successfully led the Israelites out of Egypt, through the wilderness and into their Promised Land. I believe that the God of the Israelites will lead African Americans into our Promised Land, just as he did for the Israelites. I believe that our time spent wandering through the wilderness is up, and the Promised Land of economic equality and social equity awaits our impending arrival. Our journey there will be illuminated by the internal compass of our faith.

I was born in 1983, which was the same year that Martin Luther King Day was signed into law as a federal holiday by President Ronald Reagan. When someone sees me in public they will not know my age unless I tell them. I am a progressive minded independent. They will not know my political affiliation unless I tell them. I am a Christian. They will have no clue of what my religious affiliation is based upon seeing me either. There are only two things that they will know about me without me saying a word. They will know that I am black and that I am a man. These are two things about me that will never change.

I am just like my grandfather Willie Moore; he was a black man also. He was born in 1919, on an old plantation in Scott County Mississippi. His age, his political affiliation and his religious affiliation did not matter back in the Jim Crow South. He grew up in a world in which the same men who professed the gospel of an innocent Jesus Christ on a

Sunday morning would feel no shame in the lynching of an innocent black man on a Saturday night.

My grandfather admirably served this country for four years defending the rights of foreign citizens overseas. These were rights that he was legally denied the privilege of enjoying when he returned home to Mississippi in 1946, following the end of World War II. Months after he arrived back home, he made the decision to move north as a means of escaping the dehumanization of Jim Crow segregation. He faced obstacles that I could have never imagined, all because of the fact that he was a black man. Despite those obstacles, he eventually built a good life for himself in my hometown Detroit, Michigan. He was known for being kind to others and for being the kind of man who represented the God that we serve with honor.

When he transitioned from this earth in 2004, he did not leave any money for me. There were no stocks and bonds or real estate holdings left in his will for me either. What he left for me was far greater than any tangible asset. He left for me a legacy to build upon. He accomplished a lot in his life and he made sure that he shared the key that I would need to unlock the promises of God for my own life. That important key was the example of a faith filled life. My grandfather believed that faith was the most powerful tool that I would need to succeed in my life. He believed that one day my work would touch the world.

No matter what our skin color is, we were all created equally by God. I am a person who loves people regardless of their classified race. In the years since my grandfather passed away, I have been blessed to travel all over this country sharing my gifts. I have a great responsibility to use the gifts that God has blessed me with to improve the condition of this world. As a black man; however, I have a greater responsibility to use my gifts to better the condition of black Americans.

I am often asked by my friends of European descent what it is like to be black in the United States of America. In my best way to describe it, I paint a picture that many of them have never thought to imagine. Picture if Africans decided to explore another part of the world around the turn of the 17th century. Imagine if they went to this new land and saw it as a place filled with rich fertile soil that could be used to plant crops. Feeling that they needed to find inexpensive labor to work those lands they decided to go into Europe and take its citizens as slaves and forcibly move them to the new land.

In the process of the Africans removing the European citizens from their homeland, they would also strip them of the knowledge of their country of origin, their family structures, the way in which they practiced religion and their native languages. The enslaved Europeans would have then been forced to work under dehumanizing conditions for hundreds of years without the full rights of citizenship. This mental picture that I just painted was not a reality for the Europeans but was the unfortunate reality for the sons and daughters of Africa. This is a reality that still haunts the United States of America today and continues to shape the landscape of its power structure.

The election of Donald Trump, as The President of the United States; a businessman with no prior political experience, and a documented record of discriminatory behaviors was troubling. It did not represent the end of the world however. It in fact was another sign to us that our success will come from our unity and not the actions of a political savior. Millions of Americans agree that Donald Trump is unqualified on paper to be the President of this country. For millions of them he does not represent the image of what a President should reflect. Despite those feelings we are all lawfully wedded to him in a case of political matrimony for the next several years.

President Barack Obama represented the idea of what America should be. President Donald Trump represents the reality of what America actually is. So many people today have fears of what actions President Trump may enact or what specific policies of President Obama that he may choose to dismantle. President Trump represents change that millions of Americans didn't want to believe in but ultimately have no choice but to face. As of today, we know with pretty good reasoning, what his alleged plan to Make America Great Again entails.

For those who share my ancestral DNA, America has never been great. There have been great historical moments but the consistency of its greatness has been elusive. It is a nation that was constructed by our ancestors underneath the oppressive spirit of white male supremacy. The spirit of white male supremacy and the systemic and localized racism that comes from it represent the unsealed crack in the bell of black American liberty. The election of Donald Trump was a clarion call signifying that the cavalry is not coming to save us nor is it coming to repair the unsealed crack of liberation.

The Republican Party does not seem to welcome us, The Democratic Party consistently takes us for granted and the government and corporations see us as pawns in an economic chess game that very few of the corporatocratic plutocrats desire to see us succeed within. We must look inside of ourselves for solutions. Systemic racism does have power but its power is rendered impotent when we work together with plans that pool our intellectual and financial capital. We must invest in ourselves and in one another to truly make America great.

The last several years have been marked with incidents involving police that have resulted in the deaths of several young black people in various regions of the country. There have been movements such as Black Lives Matter and Black Twitter that have been very vocal about these widespread incidents. These isolated moments must become sustained movements in order to positively change the future of the descendants of those whose forced free labor built this nation.

I grew up in Detroit, Michigan, which is statistically the most racially segregated metropolitan area in the United States of America. This segregation was accelerated as a result of the flight of white citizens across 8 Mile Road into the suburbs following the summer rebellion in July of 1967. It is a rebellion that my hometown has never recovered from. I grew up on the east side of Detroit during the height of the crack epidemic in the 1980's and 90's. I like many of the current grey-haired millennials who grew up with me witnessed murder, assaults, robbery, unlimited corner drug deals and parades of gunfire each night before bedtime.

Fortunately, amidst the chaos, I was raised in a home with mature grandparents and an insightful mother who nurtured my love of reading and writing. In the summer before my third grade year, I was tested and scored well enough to be granted the opportunity to attend a private Blue Ribbon awarded elementary and middle school in affluent Grosse Pointe Park. I soon found out that I was deemed as acting too black for my white classmate's due to the substantive nature of my words and deemed as acting too white for my black playmates, in my neighborhood, for the way in which I articulated them.

Needless to say, I had to learn to think for myself and become comfortable within my own skin many years ago. This skill has helped me tremendously in the navigation of my adulthood. Even though I grew up in an environment surrounded by poverty and crime, I never let it affect my dreams of a better life. Much of my work now is spent educating and inspiring people of all ages and races to seek God's best for their lives.

My first book, which was published in 2012, titled, *Living For Friday Dreading Sunday Night*, is a reflection of that work. This current work is also meant for everyone to enjoy but it is targeted towards African Americans and individuals that are labeled in Sociological constructs as being minorities. These individuals live in two Americas in which they strive daily to successfully strike the bicultural balance of their African identity and American citizenship. This book was not written to exclude individuals labeled by societal constructs as non-minorities. It was created to offer transparent solutions that will benefit the community from which I came. My community is often spoken at out of spite instead of spoken to out of love. This work was created with a spirit of love.

I firmly believe in the God gifted potential of black Americans. There are millions of you who have lived your lives under the umbrella of the lie of inferiority based upon the color of your skin. Millions of you have been infected from birth with the curable disease of (PTSS) Post Traumatic Slave Syndrome. This book is my God gifted prescription to cure this ailment that adversely affects so many of your lives today. The Centers for Disease Control does not have the antidote to this virus. Neither does the Mayo Clinic, nor does any pharmacy in this world.

The prescription to cure it is found within your willingness to be empowered despite a world in which some seek for you to entertain them, and others desire to see you enslaved. When I speak in terms of enslavement, I am not referring to the chattel slavery that permeated this country from the year 1619 until 1865. I am referring to the modern-day forms of slavery which includes the physical shackles provided by the prison industrial complex and the mental shackles provided by inadequate inner-city school systems, financial inequality, social inequity, fractured family structures and the low self-esteem of the collective group as a result of internalizing the lying narrative that portrays you as a second class citizen.

I do not believe that all European Americans engage in the practice of white supremacy, but I do believe that every European American benefits from the privilege afforded from its practice. I believe that the construct of white privilege in our country should be applied in a manner that benefits African Americans and other ethnic groups labeled as minorities; while we work to create our own privilege that parallels it. Our privilege will not be created based upon the supremacy of skin color, but it will be based upon the supremacy of God and the equality of humankind.

The usage of white privilege to benefit other ethnic groups is the social equivalent to a member of a warehouse club letting someone else use their membership card to gain access to discounts on products that they normally would face a much tougher effort in obtaining. The assistance of progressive minded European Americans has somewhat helped to contain the flames of racism but it will most likely not be able to fully extinguish them; due to their continuous searing engulfment of the United States of America that began long before its constitutional inception.

One of my goals for this book is for white Americans to bear clear witness to the fact that there are indeed two Americas that occupy the same geographical space in this country. I am challenging them to search both their hearts and their wallets to assist my efforts to truly make this country one nation under God, indivisible, with liberty and justice for all. I believe that each of them can use their social, political and financial resources to assist in creating the Beloved Community that Dr. Martin Luther King Jr. once spoke about. This community will not become a reality; however, until African Americans achieve financial equality and social equity to the same degree as that of European Americans.

In this book, I will explore the role of faith in the shaping of the collective destiny of African Americans in this country. I will also offer concrete solutions that will awaken the reader and inspire them to reach the Promised Land that Dr. Martin Luther King Jr. dreamed of over fifty years ago. I implore you to take what you need from it and allow it to challenge you to reach God's destiny for your life.

Chapter 1 Questions

1. What can I do to make America great?
   _____
   _____
   _____
   _____

2. In what ways can I invest in my own success?
   _____
   _____
   _____
   _____

3. In what ways can I invest in the success of the people around me?
   _____
   _____
   _____
   _____

Chapter 2

Awakening From The Dream

Over the last fifty years there has been a lot of commentary in regards to the dream of Dr. Martin Luther King Jr. There are often speeches given on the nature of it; there have also been television shows and marches to commemorate his life and the hallmarks of his beliefs. The mainstream media has focused upon the tenets of his *I Have a Dream* speech, which was given in August of 1963. These things are mostly well intentioned, but in my eyes, they miss the mark of what Dr. King was truly aiming for at the point of his untimely death on April 4th, 1968.

Dr. King in the last few speeches in his life; namely, *Where Do We Go From Here, Beyond Vietnam* and *The Other America*, focused on the plight of poor and middle-class blacks in this country. He spoke about the income disparity, the difference in the unemployment rates, the lack of money directed at majority black schools and the lack of black entrepreneurship. Dr. King understood that in order to truly be respected in this country and to become self-sufficient, blacks had to find ways to build wealth.

In his *Where Do We Go From Here* speech Dr. King stated, "With all the struggles and all the achievements, we must face the fact, however, that the Negro still lives in the basement of the Great Society. He is still at the bottom, despite the few who have penetrated to slightly higher levels." Later in his speech he stated, "Of the good things in life, the Negro has approximately one half of those of whites. Of the bad things of life, he has twice those of whites. Thus, half of all Negroes live in substandard housing. And Negroes have half the income of whites. When we turn to the negative experiences of life, the Negro has a double share: There are twice as many unemployed; the rate of infant mortality among Negroes is double that of whites."

Over fifty years after Dr. King spoke these words; much has not changed and in fact in many ways things have gotten worse. According to a 2013, Federal Reserve Bank of St. Louis study, the average median household net worth of a white family was $134,000, for an Asian family it was $91,000 and for a black family it was $11,000. These numbers are alarming and the result of the congruence of several variables.

The iron shackles of institutional racism in terms of employment and rates of pay at corporations, an unequal playing field in terms of access to quality primary and secondary education and the warehousing of a generation of young blacks into the confines of the criminal justice system are prime examples of these shackles. The latter two of my aforementioned variables work in tandem via the school-to-prison pipeline. Research has shown that future planning for prison population growth is widely attributed to the statistical projections of poorly performing students highlighted within majority black schools.

There are individuals in positions of power who desire to see black Americans as a permanent underclass, by which these economic elites can consistently profit from their misery. There is a generation of young blacks as well who have stumbled into the jagged pitfalls of this falsified narrative and internalized the incorrect belief that their skin color relegates them to a life of second class citizenship.

What Dr. King was working toward before his death was changing the mindsets of blacks within this country. In his *Where Do We Go From Here* speech; he came up with a blueprint of success for blacks. He stated, "First, we must massively assert our dignity and worth. We must stand up amid a system that still oppresses us and develop an unassailable and majestic sense of values. We must no longer be ashamed of being black. The job of arousing manhood within a people that have been taught for so many centuries that they are nobody is not easy.

The Negro must rise up with an affirmation of his own Olympian manhood. Any movement for the Negro's freedom that overlooks this necessity is only waiting to be buried. As long as the mind is enslaved, the body can never be free. Psychological freedom, a firm sense of self-esteem, is the most powerful weapon against the long night of physical slavery.

The Negro will only be free when he reaches down to the inner depths of his own being and signs with the pen and ink of assertive manhood his own emancipation proclamation. And with a spirit straining toward true self-esteem, the Negro must boldly throw off the manacles of self-abnegation and say to himself and to the world, I am somebody."

Dr. King understood that in order to narrow the wealth and achievement gap for blacks in this country, the way that they thought about themselves must be improved. The inferiority complex imprinted from the chains of slavery and Jim Crow segregation was a mental hurdle that millions of blacks were unable to overcome. Exactly fifty years after his death, the inferiority complex is still present, but it is now coupled with a sense of self-hatred that has led to the crumbling of the black family structure and the fratricide of thousands of young black people each year.

In his 1933 book titled, *The Mis-Education of The Negro*, Dr. Carter G. Woodson addressed the inferiority complex of black Americans. He wrote, "The Negro's mind has been brought under the control of his oppressor. The problem of holding the Negro down, therefore, is easily solved. When you control a man's thinking you do not have to worry about his actions. You do not have to tell him not to stand here or to go yonder. He will find his "proper place" and will stay in it. You do not need to send him to the back door. He will go without being told. In fact, if there is no door, he will cut one for his special benefit."

The Redefinition of Blackness

Your life and the contributions that you make to society matter greatly. Some people will tell you that you are inferior because of your skin color or the neighborhood where you are from. Others will say that you were not born into the right family or that your athletic ability is greater than your intellectual capacity. I say to you today, do not believe them. The negative opinions of someone else must not become the facts and standards that you adhere your own life to. Black Americans are often viewed from the perspective of commercialized stereotypes instead of as the phenomenal children of God that we actually are.

Today, the definition of blackness must be changed to represent who we actually are. A young black man should not have more street respect for spending four years or more in a penal institution as opposed to an institute for higher learning. Authentic blackness does not lose its luster within the study halls of a library and gain its shine behind the walls of a prison. Keeping it real does not involve supporting mindless and degrading music and media that have become the soundtracks and laugh tracks of our demise. Music in which the sensations of sex are promoted over the sanctity of love and media images depicting death and destruction that are promoted over images displaying self-discipline. Phrases that my generation has coined as being terms of endearment are actually linguistic Trojan horses of self-hatred that must be quarantined and disposed of away from the sacredness of our vocabularies.

No longer should we allow the young men in our families to produce children without challenging them to be active participants in the life of their child. No longer should we allow young ladies to internalize that single motherhood is a rite of passage to being an authentically strong black woman. The overconsumption of weed and alcohol should not be seen as measurements of hood authenticity. Hood authenticity should no longer be seen as a qualitative measurement of success. These and several other behaviors not mentioned are ways in which we have gotten in the way of our own progress in this society. We have lived up to the expectations of the deceased slave masters, and lived down to the promises of our ancestor's dreams.

Being black means being beautiful, it also means being creative, articulate, strong and educated. There is no room for poverty in my definition. There is no room for being uneducated in terms of ancestral history, formal education and finances. There is no room for lack of achievement. There is no room for the poor self-imaging that cultural conditioning has created. We are the head and not the tail. God created all of us equally that inhabit this earth. It does not matter our skin color or how much money we have in the bank.

I know that there is institutional racism and that the playing field is not level for blacks in this country. It has never been level and for that matter it may never become level. That does not change the fact that we must play our cards to the best of our abilities. When we play our cards, and learn to strategize together as opposed to trying to compete against and defeat each other, great things will happen for us. After a while we will transition from simply playing cards into finally dealing them.

You play your cards by maximizing your God given gifts and being the very best at whatever it is that you do. The fact that you are alive and functioning is a blessing that so many people take for granted each day. God did not create you to just come to this earth and spend your whole life fighting to survive the circumstances of it. You were created to live out a specific purpose and to be successful in doing so. I am aware of the fact that as a writer, I do not possess the power to force anyone to do anything. I do however have the ability to inspire you to believe in yourself, I can encourage you to strengthen your faith in God and I am able to provide for you a blueprint on which you can build the infrastructure of your God given dreams.

As a black male in this country, I am aware that black Americans have been masters at the art of survival for the last 400 years. Some of us have broken through the cracks of institutional racism, perceived racial inferiority and post traumatic slave syndrome to accomplish what mainstream America considers to be the indicators of success. In my first book, I referred to these individuals as Functioning Actors.

There are millions of other people currently locked outside of the gates of prosperity in which they are living impoverished due to a diverse range of issues. The varying degrees of impoverishment could be represented in the form of spiritual, psychological, physiological or economic lack. The negative social issues that we face whether they are inflicted upon us or self-inflicted, are the direct result of us not being seen through the eyes of God. How can someone claim to know God and then proceed to treat the people that they encounter as less than their equal? How can we claim to represent God and live in a manner that does not reflect Him?

The main purpose of my life is to help all of God's children appeal to and develop their higher self. I realized my purpose at the relatively young age of twenty-six. Up until that point in time, I like so many other people believed that life was only about trying to survive from one day until the next. I knew that I had God given gifts and talents but I had no outlet that would allow me to display them. I knew about God from going to church but I really didn't know Him or about His power that lived on the inside of me.

Through prayer I learned to operate with the power of my higher self. The higher self is only manifested when you see yourself through God's eyes and choose to live your life in a manner that reflects your knowledge of it. I have learned in life that unless you make plans for yourself, someone else will make plans for you. Their plans often may not be what you desire to be a part of. In order for each of us to reach our full potential in this world, the mission to simply survive in life must be abandoned. This will not be an easy task.

For black Americans, such as myself, there is nearly four hundred years of social conditioning that must be reversed for this to happen. There will be media images and low societal expectations that must be contradicted. There will also be self-defeating and impoverishing thoughts that must be eradicated as well.

It is time that we work to eliminate our debts and then transition into building tangible assets. Tangible assets include: income earning businesses, cash, stocks, bonds and real estate. This is where the real wealth lies in this country. Most of us have been taught to be consumers as opposed to being producers. When you consume and do not produce, you have no control over the means of production or ownership. Thus, you are restricted from acquiring wealth building capital. This consumer based mindset must change if we are to reach the vision of economic equality that Dr. King was reaching for. Millions of us possess the self-discipline to maintain the dreams of someone else, but lack the self-determination to create the blueprint for our own dreams. It is time for us to raise our expectations and meet them.

It is not a secret as to the reasons why, European and Asian Americans are leading in the wealth categories. Both groups place a high emphasis on self-education, formal education, occupational nepotism, entrepreneurship and building financial portfolios with tangible assets as opposed to liabilities. As black Americans, high achievement must become the rule as opposed to the exception. The blood within us once built proud civilizations in Africa. The blood within us built the infrastructure of this country, piece by piece. The blood within us fought for and won freedom and civil rights in this country. That same blood must now be put to work to reshape both our image and our destiny in this country.

The election of Donald Trump to the Presidency has placed black Americans in a precarious position. There is a sense of anxiety in our community due to his usage of inflammatory rhetoric that has awakened the slumbering dragon of right wing white American nationalism. For us it represents a clear reminder that we cannot rely upon the government to be our savior.

President Obama did the best job that he could while in office. His Presidential legacy may have lifted the social and political boats of a select few groups with a rising tide, but his presence did little to free black America from the tethering anchor of historical oppression. That task is one that each of us must shoulder together. It may seem like an impossible situation to overcome, but with God's help there is no great thing that cannot be done.

Chapter 2 Questions

1. What does Dr. King's dream look like in my eyes?

   _____
   _____
   _____
   _____

2. Do I know that God loves me?

   _____
   _____
   _____
   _____

3. Do I believe that God created everyone equally?

   _____
   _____
   _____
   _____

Chapter 3

Where Is Our Joshua?

For black Americans, Dr. King represented what Moses was to the Israelites in the Bible. Moses led the Israelites to the doorstep of the Promised Land, but he was unable to lead them into it. Joshua, his successor, led his people into it. For black Americans today, our Joshua has not stepped forward as of yet. Exactly fifty years after the death of our Moses, millions of us still encircle the Promised Land of economic equality and social equity still unable to enter into it. There are a myriad of factors that have led to this group level abstinence from the Promised Land. Chief among them are institutional racism and the internalized psychological effects of post traumatic slave syndrome within the black community.

    A great majority of us know that as long as the United States Government and the puppet masters of social-engineering (i.e. The Bilderberg Group, The World Bank Group, The International Monetary Fund, Kappa Beta Phi) and other groups that hold the real power in this country continue to have their way, black Americans will never have a Joshua. Any single individual who actually dares to organize us to pool our resources and create progressive minded change will likely be assassinated, imprisoned or severely marginalized.

I have a strong desire to see black Americans achieve the dreams that Dr. King spoke about in his speeches, *Where Do We Go From Here, Beyond Vietnam* and *The Other America*. The media corporatocracy will act as if the years 1964-1968 did not exist in the life of Dr. King. They will continue to sell you on the tenets of his *I Have a Dream Speech* and simultaneously promote the economic nightmare of inequality. They will act as if Malcolm X never gave the speech titled *Who Taught You to Hate Yourself*. Let's be honest, they act as if Malcolm X never existed and desire for you to share that belief as well.

Unless black Americans learn about our true ancestral history before European colonization, we will continue struggling to succeed in this country as a collective. Unless we pool our economic resources and adopt a mentality that places a higher value on ownership over consumerism, we will continue struggling to succeed as a collective group. Our great-grandparents were forced to work for free as slaves. Our grandparents worked as sharecroppers in those same fields as a means to survive. We owe it them to now to seek to gain controlling interest in the areas in which we labor.

Unless we begin to value formal and self-education, we will not succeed as a collective. Unless we organize the energy of the police brutality protests into voter registration drives and much higher participation in local and mid-term elections, we will never succeed as a collective. Unless we field strong candidates, whose mission is to see the ultimate success of our people instead of appeasing the corporate puppet masters, lobbying firms and special interest groups, we will never succeed as a collective. Until we learn to see our individual selves and each other through the eyes of almighty God, we will never succeed as a collective.

The Success of Other Groups

The mental wounds of post traumatic slave syndrome are too real and too relevant to ignore. A majority of the most pressing issues permeating within our community are the psychological outflow of social conditioning. The great lesson of the lives of Dr. King and Malcolm X is that oftentimes when the leader of a movement is silenced, the movement is silenced with them. For us to reach the Promised Land as a collective, we need a unified agenda. Do Gay and Lesbian Americans have a leader? Do Asian Americans have a leader? Do Ashkenazi Jewish Americans have a leader? None of these aforementioned groups has a central leader. What they do have are organized human networks, think tanks, economic solidarity and a sense of communal unity.

The success of these groups has laid out the road map that we can follow to transition from survival mindedness to successful living. Look at the legislative and judicial victories that these groups routinely have. Their strength and power is rooted in their cohesive ability to network for the betterment of their communities.

From a young woman named Paige, I learned that Ashkenazi Jewish Americans engage in a practice called Jewish Geography. When a member of their community meets another person from their community, they ask one another questions in order to determine if they have mutual friends or relatives. This is an important method that helps them network inside of their community and serves as a means to consistently keep their community strong both socially and economically.

In order for us to overcome police brutality, fratricide, underachievement, regressive public policy and the prison industrial complex, it is incumbent upon black Americans to do the same thing. We don't need one Joshua. We just need several million of us who can look in the mirror and believe that the redefinition of blackness begins with them. The words that God gave to Joshua are an excellent guide. "Have I not commanded you? Be strong and of good courage; do not be afraid, nor be dismayed, for the Lord your God is with you wherever you go" (Joshua 1:8-9).

Our standards must be raised if we are to thrive within this country. Our own Black Wall Street in Tulsa, Oklahoma of one-hundred years ago, along with the present day Asian---American and Ashkenazi---Jewish---American community models should be our blueprints. These listed communities place a very high value on self and formal-education, they value patronizing one another in business and they possess a shared sense of communal unity. They are the examples that we must emulate in order to find collective success for ourselves in this country.

I understand that neither of the latter two mentioned groups bears the brunt of white supremacy that blacks do in this country (See Tulsa Riots 1921). I understand that neither of them have the same level of psychological and economic restrictions that many of us and our ancestors have had to deal with in this country. That does not mean that we cannot dare to dream bigger dreams. That does not mean that we cannot make the choice to start valuing self- and formal education over entertainment and investments over consumerism. These choices are in our hands.

We are responsible for our own destiny in this country. No individual on this earth is supreme over you black America. We are God's original creation. He didn't make anyone on this earth superior or inferior to another human. All we have are positive or negative choices that affect us as individuals and as a collective community. The oppression of chattel slavery sought to make us think as individuals only and forsake our group. Now we must begin to think of the betterment of our group for the sake of our individuality.

Black Lives Do Matter

The inconvenient and controversial truth is that black lives, especially those of black males, are not seen as being valuable in this country. The standard was set when the toes of the first captive Africans landed in Jamestown, Virginia in 1619. White supremacy was the standard then and has systematically been woven into the fabric of our country over the last 400 years. A by-product of it is the sense of self-hatred that many black Americans feel toward themselves and each other.

Today, black life in this country is seen as having little to no value unless it is creating greater wealth for European American corporate masters or providing them with entertainment. There are a group of blacks in this country that have internalized the images of themselves that the fabric of white supremacy has presented to them. They are the Buffalo Soldiers from the platoon of perceived black American inferiority. They are the individuals who stand on guard at the bedside of the soon to be deceased system of white supremacy. These individuals choose to identify themselves as a part of the mainstream culture of America and disassociate themselves away from the myriad of issues that black Americans face in this country as a collective group. Some of them even take pleasure in the parroting of political talking points that denigrate black-Americans.

They do this as a means to profit and increase their social and political profiles. They also choose to stay silent about important topics such as discrimination, reparations, social inequity, economic inequality and the success of the pre-colonial kingdoms of Africa. Most of them are good God-fearing people that I do indeed love despite our noted ideological and political differences. On the contrary, the individuals that speak about the aforementioned topics are often silenced, marginalized as militant agitators, or labeled as non-conformists.

The Decriminalization of Blackness

Then there is the second group of blacks in this country that have internalized the images of themselves that the fabric of white supremacy has presented to them. Many of them have spent their lives placing entertainment over education. They live down to the projected standards of inferiority that white supremacy has demanded of them. They have often taken the bait of drugs and made other poor decisions that have landed them in prison, caskets or recording studios peddling community and mind numbing musical lyrics for their corporate masters. So many of them are clueless to the fact of how much their lives truly matter. They must learn to view their lives from the perspective of the God that created each of us.

Unfortunately, their image is what many whites and police officers fear when they come in contact with a young black person that they do not know personally. They are seen as the representatives of our community. Their images have most law abiding young black people seen as aimless, blood thirsty, uneducated and unmotivated menaces to society. They are pawns on the chessboard of Wall Street profits. Whether it is as pawns for the prison systems, (cheap convict labor) or the police, (new high tech military weaponry) the news media, (high ratings based on stoking racial tensions) or the record companies, (mind numbing music that is often the soundtrack to the prison industrial complex).

The great and simultaneously daunting thing about what I wrote in the previous paragraph is that we as black Americans have the power to change each of those things for the better. Racism and white supremacy is a multi-trillion-dollar business conglomerate that has been going strong for over 400 years. We must make it our business as black Americans to put it out of business to the best of our abilities.

In my mind black on black crime is just as upsetting as another person outside of our race killing our people. It should equally upset you as well. I hear it often questioned as to why black Americans seem to find an allied sense of community when someone outside of our ethnic group kills a member of our group.

This is due to the mindset of protecting the tribe from those outside the margins of our ethnic group. It is similar to family members picking on each other but being ready to go to war if someone outside of the family tried to pick on someone within their family dynamic. It is undoubtedly hypocritical and causes us to appear to be inconsistent in our abhorrence for senseless violence. It is very similar to us calling ourselves the word nigga and then being upset that whites call us the word nigger. The former and the latter words both define ignorance. The usage of the former displays self-hatred and the usage of the latter is hatred directed squarely at us. Love is absent from both.

I understand white supremacy and the institutional racism that it manifests upon our community. Yes, the government (See Nicaraguan Contra Scandal) is partly responsible for the guns and drugs that have infiltrated our communities since the 1970's. The truth is it is equally our fault if we use the guns or sell them in our neighborhoods. It is our fault if we use the drugs or sell them in our neighborhoods. Just because it's there does not mean that we should partake in it. No one has a vested interest in coming to help us out of the mess that we have had a hand in creating.

The Republicans use us as punching bags and the Democrats use us as bean bags on which they rest their feet. The Republicans oppress us with malfeasant public policy and the Democrats impress us with lies and stomach teasing crumbs from the master's table. Marching demands the attention of politicians and has done so for many years in this country. In the Presidential era of Donald Trump, garnering attention is not sufficient unless it is followed by progressive implementation of policies that meet our needs.

I certainly believe in conveying messages of truth to individuals in positions of power, but our messages are ultimately powerless to change our circumstances without our creation of concrete plans to prosper ourselves. This will not be an easy journey into the Promised Land of equality, but it is a journey that I believe we will ultimately succeed in accomplishing.

Non-Violent Revolution

In the same manner as Dr. King, I believe that for black Americans, the pathway to our successful entry into the Promised Land of economic equality and social equity must be paved with the usage of non-violent tactics. In the Bible, when Joshua led the Israelites into the Promised Land, they employed a military strategy in which violence was used as their primary method of entry. This method of operation is not wise nor is it an effective strategy for black Americans to use today. We are thoroughly outnumbered and severely outgunned in this country. To enter into our Promised Land our strategy for success must be powered by the resolute strength of our minds and not by the might of our weaponry.

There may be some people reading this book that may have fanatical notions about launching a violent revolution as a means to level the playing field for black Americans. In our shared anguish in response to the lack of convictions of law enforcement agents in the killings of unarmed black Americans, I have heard many people speak glowingly about it. I understand their pain, but I do not agree with their proposed strategies. I believe that we have the right to defend ourselves if our lives are placed in imminent danger, but the need for self-defense and the desire to engage in a violent revolution are two separate organisms.

I firmly believe that a violent revolution will only dilute the potency of our cause and not lead to the social progress that we desire to see during our lifetime on this earth. It is imperative that black Americans keep in mind, that the inhabitants of mainstream America are children of God just as we are; no matter how some of them may view us. In order to reach the Promised Land of economic equality and social equity, we must choose to employ a revolution led by our intellect, which will feature the usage of our activated brainpower over that of our gunpowder. In subsequent chapters, I will share the strategies that I believe will lead us toward the successful implementation of our intellectual revolution.

Chapter 3 Questions

1. What does my Promised Land resemble?

   _____
   _____
   _____
   _____

2. What must I do to reach God's Promised Land for my life?

   _____
   _____
   _____
   _____

3. How can I assist someone else in reaching their Promised Land?

   _____
   _____
   _____
   _____

Chapter 4

The Price of Freedom

During the Reconstruction Era, immediately following the Civil War, African Americans made measurable progress in the political and economic arenas in this country. They began to work collectively amongst themselves to improve their quality of life. I believe that this past progress offers us a glimpse of what can be achieved today if African Americans take a unified approach in relation to economics and politics in our community. I firmly believe the success that was experienced after coming out of slavery is an essential ingredient in the recipe of prosperity for African Americans today.

In the twelve-year Reconstruction Era from 1865-1877, African Americans possessed marketable skills that afforded for them the opportunity to provide a good quality of life for themselves without the influence of their former slave masters. These became prosperous times for some of the newly freed blacks. Many of them were able to own their own homes and land for the first time in their lives. Some of them even purchased the homes and lands of their former slave masters. A great number of them became economically successful business owners and some were even elected as state and federal legislators.

Also, during this same time period, using the money generated from federal land sales; the US government paved the way for land grant colleges to be created. Several of these schools became what we refer to in modern times as historically black colleges. This was made possible by the passage of the Morril Act in 1862, which promoted the creation of higher educational institutions that specialized in agricultural and mechanical arts.

The recently freed black Americans were also granted protection by the United States military in the South. They needed this protection due to the constant threats that they faced from domestic terrorist organizations such as the Ku Klux Klan, The Knights of the White Camelia, The Red Shirts and The White League. These organizations were founded based upon the anger of former Confederate soldiers, who were upset over losing the Civil War, and the progressive societal changes that resulted from that loss. The former Confederate soldiers, and their supporters, were angry at seeing the new freedom and prosperity of black-Americans. The primary objective of their organizations was to emphatically restore the system of white supremacy in the southern states by terrorizing the recently freed black Americans and denying their civil rights.

Ultimately, the period of individual and collective prosperity following the Civil War experienced by southern black Americans did not last. Its untimely demise was met following a political disagreement related to electoral-college votes immediately following the 1876 Presidential election. The brutal aftermath of this political disagreement between The Republican Party candidate Rutherford B. Hayes, and The Democratic Party candidate Samuel Tilden would place the civil liberties of southern black Americans into a politically induced coma that would last for nearly 100 years.

In the election of 1876, Tilden won the popular vote, but there was a dispute in several southern states relating to the number of electoral-college votes that Hayes received. Seeking to remedy the political conflict, a meeting was held in February of 1877, at the Wormley Hotel in Washington D.C. As a result of that meeting, a deal was brokered between the two main political parties that would have devastating effects on the lives of African Americans. That deal which is often referred to as "The Compromise of 1877," gave Rutherford B. Hayes the presidency and called for the United States military to leave their posts in the former Confederate states.

With the removal of US military protection, African Americans became sitting ducks inside a polluted pond of social oppression. Southern states subsequently began to exercise their rights with feelings of impunity from the United States government. Blacks all over the south began to suffer from the unregulated effects of domestic terrorism at the hands of the children of the Confederacy. The system of white supremacy began to gain its footing once again, and Jim Crow laws began to take effect in the South. These laws were put in place to create a legalized caste system that would unjustly keep African Americans underneath their control as legalized second class citizens.

The Jim Crow laws were designed to segregate blacks in a separate and unequal social order. Many blacks were threatened with violence or suffered from it by doing things such as simply registering to vote or owning their own businesses. A great number of black land owners had their properties taken through both terroristic threats and legal improprieties.

Blacks who valiantly fought against injustices were often accused of and/or convicted of phantom offenses.

Some of those who were accused or convicted often found themselves imprisoned. They became legalized slaves to their states of residence and leased laborers for former slave masters and corporations. Others who fought against injustice were often lynched without legal provocation. Their lives were not seen as being valuable and the sacrifices that they made in their effort to experience true freedom are often relegated to the concealed pages of American history. Black Americans living in the 21st century must always remember the down payment for freedom that our ancestors once paid on our behalf. The reminders of our current due balance seem to alert us with each recurrence of injustice displayed in our modern day news cycle.

Freedom in The 21st Century

When the not guilty verdict was delivered in the George Zimmerman murder trial on Saturday, July 13th 2013, I felt as if my country had just been set back fifty years. I was hurt, angry and greatly disappointed by the injustice that I believed was unfairly rendered in a Florida courtroom. Many people wondered, myself included, how could a grown man racially profile, stalk and then proceed to act as a judge, jury and executioner to a child that he had not previously met? How could a jury of six women, not sort through the inconsistencies of Zimmerman's story and then be manipulated into believing that the victim was the perpetrator and that the perpetrator was a victim?

I remember asking myself back then, how can this happen in 2013? One hundred and forty-eight years after my ancestors were freed. Fifty-eight years after the brutal lynching of Emmitt Till, the key event that sparked the Civil Rights Movement. Forty-nine years after the Civil Rights Act was signed into law, and only forty-eight years after the Voting Rights Act was signed into law. I felt the same emotions on May 18th 2017, when a not guilty verdict was rendered on behalf of former Tulsa Police Officer Betty Shelby, who was shown on video shooting an unarmed black man named Terence Crutcher, who at the time he was shot was posing no threat to her.

In the years between the Zimmerman and Shelby verdicts, miscarriages of justice and the killings of unarmed black men on video seemed to sadly become a common occurrence. All of this was happening with the first black President occupying the highest political office in this country. This dichotomy is clear-cut evidence of how far we have come and proof of how much further we still have to go.

Today, as I write this, I ponder two questions. The first is, are we as black Americans truly free? The second is, if we are not free what is binding us and how can we break free? To answer my first question, we as black-Americans are legally free by law. The ratification of the Thirteenth Amendment established this fact on December 6th, 1865.

As for being wanted here in this country and being respected as equals by the individuals that wield economic and political power, the jury of inequality renders that guilty verdict daily. With each senseless act of violence heaped upon us by those empowered to protect us, it speaks loudly and clearly. It speaks with the same pitch and tenor as the bullets that ended the lives of Emmitt Till, Medgar Evers, Malcolm X and Dr. Martin Luther King Jr. The same pitch and tenor that floods drugs into inner cities, young men into the prison industrial complex and the mass media images and sounds that undervalue, degrade and marginalize our people.

We must realize that there was never a plan for us within the United States outside of the confines of slavery. Our ancestors were human commodities that were sold and traded at will. Their worth was determined by demand for items such as silver pounds and sugar before US currency was established. How much are you worth today? Who are you permitting to determine your value?

There is a difference between being free and being on equal footing. There are two things that are respected in this country. The first is economic power. The second is political power. Economic power now more than ever influences politics. Please see the Supreme Court's partial repeal of the Voting Rights Act in June 2013, and its Citizens United decision in January 2010, which essentially gives corporations limitless spending on political elections. Also see special interest groups such as The American Legislative Exchange Council, The John Birch Society, The Heritage Foundation and The Cato Institute, which influence policy decisions on both the state and federal level. These groups have spawned things such as Florida's Stand Your Ground Law and Citizens United among other pieces of legislation that harm minorities along with the poor and middle class.

For many black people that live in this country, the miscarriages of justice that repeatedly happened during the latter stages of the Obama Presidential Administration were the confirmation of several things. It confirmed in many of our minds that no matter how kind we are, no matter our level of education, occupation, how much money we earn or awards we receive, that there will always be those in society that still see us as three fifths human. Some of us have internalized this unequal ratio and have spent our lives living down to the level of it. My word to those brothers and sisters that are doing that is simple. Please leave that way of thinking and living in the past. It is now over and you are free to live to the level that God created you to do so.

Look at your cable or satellite package of channels. You may have over 300 channels. How many of those channels are black owned entities that show black people in a positive light? There are only four prominent channels that I can think of. The OWN network, which is owned by Oprah Winfrey, TV One which, is owned by Cathy Hughes, Aspire, which is owned by Magic Johnson, and Bounce TV which features Ambassador Andrew Young and Martin Luther King III in its ownership group. It is a sad set of circumstances when we have within this nation over forty million black Americans with over one trillion dollars in capital, unwilling to work together. We have neglected to use our money, resources and intellect collectively. It is up to us to use what we have to bring about positive changes within our communities.

Colin Kaepernick

During the 2016 NFL football season, San Francisco 49ers quarterback Colin Kaepernick began kneeling during the pregame playing of the national anthem. His silent form of protest represented a salient attempt to bring awareness to the social injustices that disproportionately affect black Americans. The reactions to his protest proved that there are indeed two America's that black Americans work daily to balance our lives in. Polls showed that a majority of black---Americans understood the motivation---behind---Kaepernick's protest. Many white Americans who identify themselves politically as liberals or progressives seemed to also understand the reasoning behind his protest as well.

For a large number of conservative white Americans and conservative black Americans, Kaepernick's protest--was deemed as being unpatriotic and a misguided attempt to distract from the business of football operations. Many of them see him as a divisive figure who they feel should just focus on playing football and live in perpetual silence in regards to modern day social issues. I do not agree with their assessment of Kaepernick. I believe that he is a man who was bold in his attempt to shed light upon subjects that are of utter importance to black Americans.

When black Americans routinely see people that look like ourselves killed on camera by people that are paid by our tax dollars to protect us, it is alarming. When we then see those same individuals acquitted of those killings, it causes us to feel outraged and leaves us questioning the validity of our own lives. We live with the knowledge that our names could easily be the next one trending as a social media displayed hashtag or our faces could just as easily be prominently displayed on a t-shirt.

Some individuals reading this will question me about the outrage that black Americans feel when fratricide is committed in our own community. Some will point to the example of the high murder rate in the city of Chicago the last several years. My answer to them is this: When black Americans kill one another, we go to prison for our crimes. Take for example the state of Illinois where the city of Chicago is located.

In the year 2016, there were a total of 44,817 inmates incarcerated in the state of Illinois. Of those inmates, 8,744 or 19.5% of them were incarcerated for homicide. There were a total of 25,398 black inmates incarcerated in the state. This number represented 56.7% of the total inmate population in the state.

The state of Illinois represents the disparity that is seen in the inmate population all over this country. As of December 31st, 2015, there were approximately 1,476,847 prisoners in the United States of America. There were 1,298,159 inmates in state prisons excluding Nevada and Oregon, which were the only states that did not submit their information to the bureau of justice. There were also 178,688 inmates in federal prisons as well. There were a total of 523,000 black inmates in the United States serving time in both federal and state run correctional facilities. This number represents approximately 35.4% of the overall prison population. Black Americans comprise less than 15% of the United States population and make up 35.4% of the overall inmate population. This statistical evidence proves that when crimes are committed in this country and are both justly and unjustly attributed to black Americans, we disproportionately go to prison for them.

Colin Kaepernick used his platform as an athlete to shed light upon these disparities that are often found to be buried in the sullen graveyard of empirical data away from the political talking point consciousness of mainstream America. For the usage of his platform, he has sacrificed millions of dollars and remained an unsigned free agent throughout the 2017 NFL football season. His plight is clear evidence of the price that black Americans are often forced to pay when we boldly speak the self-evidence of our truths to the body politic of the mainstream American power structure.

The aforementioned power structure applauds loudly for us when we run for yardage on a football field but will question our credentials when we desire to run for political office. That same structure will cheer for us when we reach for the goal line on a football field but will question our motives when we reach for the goal line of economic equality, when we buy interest in companies or form our own corporations. The structure will shout jubilantly when we intercept a pass on the football field and take it back to the house for a touchdown, but will question our sanity when we seek to intercept the errant passes of social inequity that disproportionately target our community.

The stars and stripes of the American Flag are supposed to represent the freedom of all Americans. For black Americans, in the last 242 years since Betsy Ross designed it, the flag has not lived up to the words that were constituted in the US Constitution and declared in the Declaration of Independence. For a large number of mainstream Americans, as long as black Americans are playing sports or providing entertainment we are only then seen as being valuable components to the power structure of America.

I am not a professional athlete and if I was, I would be close to my retirement as a player. I like to laugh and joke at times and maybe even sing a little, but I am not an entertainer. I am an educated black man in America who has learned how to incorporate the will of God for my life through the ink of my pen. I know the price that I may have to pay for writing a book such as this one that is designed to uplift the economic mindset and societal self-esteem of black Americans.

I have written this book without the fear of what may come my way. I am not afraid to put my John Hancock on this literary Declaration of Independence away from the 400-year oligarchical reign of the American caste system of white supremacy. This is due to my faith in the God of Abraham. He has guided me during my entire lifetime and He has equipped me with the power of His spirit. Colin Kaepernick was not afraid to take a knee in order to bring awareness to the plight of the other America. For him it represented his tithe into the collection plate of true black American freedom. This book and the speeches that I give in relation to it represent my contribution into that same plate.

Whether it is your influence, your money, your vote or your intellectual capital, we need your contribution as well. That is the true price of freedom and it will cover the expenses that we will undoubtedly incur on our journey to the Promised Land of economic equality and social equity in this country. It is a cost that we must remunerate on behalf of our descendants.

The energy and collective spirit that millions of us have had since the July 2013, legal acquittal of George Zimmerman, is the exact fuel that we need to drive in a new way of living. Each of us must look in the mirror and figure out the greatness that we possess inside of us as individuals. We must answer the following questions: How can I make my life and the lives of those around me much better? How can I inspire someone around me? When these questions are truthfully answered and focused action is placed behind them, things will begin to change for the better. A domino like effect will be produced that will foster an undercurrent of positive change all around this country.

The Emancipated Mind

The greatest investment that you will make is not found in the stock market. It is not found in real estate or in any commodity that can be bought, sold or traded. The greatest personal investment that a person can ever make is what they invest into their mind. During the time of chattel slavery, reading and writing was a punishable offense if slaves were found to be partaking in it. The reason this was a punishable offense was due to the slave masters fear of the slaves emancipating their minds from the systematic manipulation of their masters.

The educated slave was deemed as being difficult to control and was considered to be a threat to the status quo of plantation operations. I am of the firm belief that readers are indeed leaders. The educational system in this country does not encourage individuals to think critically. We are taught in a manner that values standardized test scores over individual aptitude. I wholly understand the value of formal education, but self-education is a lifelong journey.

Scores of individuals make the decision to limit their reading after they complete their formal education. Many neglect to focus on learning or self-improvement and get sucked into only focusing upon surviving life one day at a time. There are so many people that have lived for years on end without seeking to improve their level of knowledge. If we as black Americans are to reach our God gifted potential, this certainly must change. Our community is in need of more knowledge, wisdom and strength. Each of them must be activated and applied. There is no use in having knowledge, wisdom and strength if they are unable to be applied.

If you would like to get started on your quest to gain more knowledge, wisdom and strength there are several sources that I recommend. The first and most important source in my mind is the Bible. Please read the book of Genesis from chapters 37-50 regarding the life of Joseph. Another great place to read is the book of Joshua, which tells the story of the Israelites finally entering into the Promised Land after 40 years of wandering through the wilderness. I will explore in greater depth the stories of both Joseph and the Israelites later in this book. I also recommend the books listed in the box below to assist you in elevating the way you think about yourself.

Christopher Columbus and the Afrikan Holocaust by Dr. John Henrik Clarke
Secret of The Ages by Robert Collier
The Wealth Choice by Dr. Dennis Kimbro
Before The Mayflower by Lerone Bennett Jr.
Black Labor White Wealth by Dr. Claud Anderson
Life Visioning by Dr. Michael Beckwith
Outwitting The Devil by Napoleon Hill

Essentials for Success

In my mind, there are three important things that are lacking within the black community as a whole. They are as follows: applied wisdom, definiteness of purpose and a sense of communal unity. The most important attribute that every successful person must have is wisdom. In the book of Proverbs chapter 1 verse 7 it reminds us that "the fear of the Lord is the beginning of knowledge, but fools despise wisdom and instruction." Proverbs chapter 2 verse 6 goes on to say, "For the Lord gives wisdom; From His mouth come knowledge and understanding."

In the black community and in our nation as a whole, the fear of God is missing. It has been replaced by the fear of other people's opinions. In my mind, the fear of other people's opinions is the beginning of all foolishness. Foolishness is the polar opposite of wisdom. In our community, we must begin to think higher thoughts in regards to our own lives and those around us.

In terms of definiteness of purpose, each of us must set individual success goals for our own lives and earnestly work to meet them. This is where we must take formal and self-education more seriously than we do sports and entertainment. In terms of unity, we must find the resolve to work together toward common sense solutions that uplift our people and portray us in a much more positive light. Examples of this are shown in the box below.

Begin to view yourself and others through the eyes of God.
Learn to be comfortable in your own skin and permit God's spirit to guide your decisions instead of the opinions of others.
Begin to treat every day as a gift and live with a sense of definite purpose.
Start your own businesses and support the efforts of one another in enterprise.
Vote in local elections and national mid-term elections for candidates that have detailed plans that feature measures that will produce upward economic mobility for the black community, the poor and the middle class. (Consider 3rd party Candidates)
Run for political office yourself or support viable

> progressive minded candidates that care more about doing the will of the people than that of lobbyists.
>
> Mentor an at risk young person in your family or community circle that lacks proper guidance. (Attempt to repair fractured family structures)
>
> Challenge music artists and record labels to clean up their music that often portrays black Americans as uncivilized savages.
>
> Challenge television and film studios to produce positive shows and films that paint black Americans in a positive light as opposed to negative stereotypical images.
>
> Support industries and companies that invest their time, money and energy into improving the quality of our communities.

These steps will help remedy the mental, spiritual and economic poverty that plagues our community. This will in turn loosen the grip that the prison industrial complex has on our community. At this juncture in our history it is critical that we bury the inner racial division that has kept us from working together for the betterment of our people. There are no superheroes coming to rescue us from the lonely road to perdition. It is up to us to seek the wisdom of God and begin to reshape the destiny of the descendants of those whose forced labor built this country. It is going to take a rainbow coalition of love to make lasting change.

We need the support of people from all races and all faiths. Nevertheless, the vital changes that we need must first begin with us as black Americans. I am confident that I am a part of the Joshua generation that will reach the Promised Land that Dr. Martin Luther King Jr. once spoke about. Let us cross the Jordan River of inequality together, using a bridge built with the materials of wisdom, defined purpose and unity. In the words of God's servant Joshua, "Sanctify yourselves, for tomorrow the Lord will do wonders among you" (Joshua 3:5).

Chapter 4 Questions

1. Do I know God's purpose for my life?
   _____
   _____
   _____
   _____

2. Am I currently walking in God's purpose for my life?
   _____
   _____
   _____
   _____

3. Do I value lifelong learning?
   _____
   _____
   _____
   _____

Chapter 5

Our Image and Our History

There are a great number of black Americans who believe that our ancestors were nothing more than slaves and uncivilized savages that the European slave traders discovered living in the jungles of West Africa. This psychological construct has led to many of them accepting that label and unable to connect with the spirit of God within them. This is a result of not being taught about the success of pre-colonial Africans and believing that God looks nothing like them and therefore does not care about them as much as He does for others. This incorrect mindset must change if they are going to reach their God gifted potential in this world.

In the book of Genesis, we read about God's creation of mankind. Then God said, "Let Us make man in Our image, according to Our likeness; let them have dominion over the fish of the sea, over the birds of the air, and over the cattle, over all the earth and over every creeping thing that creeps on the earth." So, God created man in His own image; in the image of God He created him; male and female He created them" (Genesis 1:26-27).

I would like to first say that I am unashamedly black and unapologetically Christian. I am also proud of my African genealogy. I am a man who prays and keeps God first place in my life. With that said, there is an issue that must be addressed. This issue albeit controversial is very relevant as to what has shaped the belief systems and attitudes of millions of people.

If you ever walk into a church that espouses the belief in a religion called Christianity, there is a historical figure named Yeshua, who is at the center of it. He is more commonly known by the English language translation of His name, Jesus Christ. He lived approximately 2,000 years ago in an area that is geographically in Western Asia. This area is currently referred to as the Middle Eastern region of the world. There are no photographic images of Jesus, since cameras did not exist during the time period that He lived on earth. The Bible describes Him as having hair like wool and feet like fine brass (Revelation 1:14-15). This image described by John the Apostle, the noted author of the book of Revelation, contradicts the popular image of Jesus that is displayed around the world.

The image of a European Jesus with Nordic facial features is widely credited to Italian painter and sculptor Leonardo Da Vinci. His world-famous painting titled, *The Last Supper*, was completed in the year 1498. This image has been used as the accepted societal depiction of what Jesus is believed to resemble for over 500 years and counting. If you look at the people who currently live where Jesus resided nearly 2,000 years ago, they do not resemble the figure of Jesus from the Da Vinci painting or the media images of Him that are prominently displayed in

Christian films, literature and in history books all over the world. I believe that this was done by design and not by default.

The Nordic image of Jesus has been used as means to subconsciously condition the world to the incorrect belief that European males by nature of their birth are the ultimate reflection of God. This centuries old lie has been used to justify the practice of white male supremacy and perpetuate the argument that individuals with melanin in their skin are inferior to them. A chief component of the concept of white supremacy is that black relevancy must first be validated by whites before it is deemed to be legitimate. The fact that former President Barack Obama had to prove both his citizenship and his Christianity is evidence of this. It was akin to a freed black man being forced to show his freedom papers to whites during the time of chattel slavery.

As a trained social scientist, I understand the power of social engineering and mental conditioning. If something is repeated long enough and often enough, it will eventually become ingrained within the fabric of a society. The mental conditioning of the European image of Jesus has led to many people falsely believing that He and the white male are synonymous. I am here to break the news that they are not one in the same. Despite what people may believe or what they may say, no one living on this earth knows with certainty what Jesus actually looks like.

Some people reading this are currently wondering if the image of Jesus truly matters. I believe that there is over 500 years of empirical evidence that says it does indeed matter. The image of Jesus does not matter in terms of our love for Him, but it instead matters in relation to our own self-image. What if Da Vinci would have painted an image of Jesus with dark skin and Negroid facial features? This would have most likely presented a roadblock to the justification of the Trans-Atlantic slave trade. It would have presented a challenge for the European slave traders to convince the enslaved Africans that they were inferior human beings if the image of God looked similar to that of their own.

There are many people who would lead you to believe, that Jesus, if He lived in our society today, would be a politically conservative white male from the heartland of America. They believe that He would speak of the virtues of the free market economy and place His emphasis on combatting wedge social issues such as abortion and gay marriage. They also believe that He would pay lip service to the poor and downtrodden members of our society, by extolling to them about the values and merits of individual achievement.

This image of Jesus does not fit the description of the man who is depicted in the Bible that Christians such as myself, consider to be our sacred text. The man who I read about came to earth to serve the poor and to give His life as a ransom for the sins of humankind. The European image of Jesus represents the idol worshiping of a graven image. It has also caused inner faith division amongst Christians and bolstered the incorrect narrative of racial supremacy predicated upon the skin color of human beings. Most notably, that same image has also served as the drum major for the myth of divine white skinned righteousness. African Americans have unfortunately spent the last five centuries marching incorrectly to its cadence.

In our society imagery is very important in terms of shaping our belief systems. I grew up believing that Jesus Christ was a European male with Caucasoid facial features. This subconsciously led me to believe that people with white skin represented the earthly reflection of God. It also led me to incorrectly believe that by virtue of me being born with dark skin, that I was somehow inferior to the people with white skin. I also incorrectly believed that since most of the black people that I saw around me were poor and that most of the white people around me were upper middle class and wealthy, that it somehow made them better than me.

In my mind back then, I incorrectly reasoned that since I descended from slaves and I believed that Jesus was a white male just as the slave masters were, by virtue of my birth, I wrongly believed that I was born into a permanent underclass. I didn't realize that everything that I was taught in school was from the perspective of the European male. My concept of world history, religion, economics, media imagery and standards of beauty were all from that perspective. Most importantly, I believed that Jesus was a European white male and that if a white male was not in a position of power then the concepts presented or the organization somehow lacked legitimacy. I believe that some of you reading this may have grown up feeling that way as well.

I believed in white supremacy and black inferiority because I simply did not know any better and I was not taught anything different to contradict my knowledge at that time. I knew nothing about black history outside of the struggles of slaves and the fight for Civil Rights in the 20th Century. Each of those historical developments fed my incorrect belief in white supremacy by fostering my belief that in order for black people to gain measurable levels of progress within this country, a well-meaning white person must first open up the door of opportunity for us. It taught me that if a black male were to stand up and demand to be treated fairly in this country, that he would be labeled a malcontent and be seen as a threat to the welfare of society. It took me a lot of years to reverse this conditioning within my mind. I had to discover the truth by doing independent research.

In my research, I uncovered the correlation between the short-sighted Eurocentric perspective of Christianity and its flawed foundation which was built upon the system of capitalism. Late Kenyan President Jomo Kenyatta once spoke openly about this correlation and its impact upon his country. He is quoted as stating, "When the missionaries arrived, the Africans had the land and the missionaries had the Bible. They taught us how to pray with our eyes closed. When we opened them, they had the land and we had the Bible."

My Christian Journey

When a person controls your concept of God it is their entry point into them controlling your mind. There were many black Americans in the 20th Century, who left the faith of Christianity and converted to Islam based upon their disdain for the Eurocentric brand of Christianity that the United States was founded upon. This brand of Christianity was practiced by slave traders and shaped the theological constructs of the United States of America.

Some of those constructs included the false narratives that Jesus Christ was a European and that dark skinned people by virtue of their birth were forced to live under the curse of Ham. Ham was the son of Noah who was cursed for uncovering the nakedness of his father as depicted in the book of Genesis (See Genesis 9:20-27). These false narratives, amongst others, allowed European Americans to live unashamedly with the cognitive dissonance of writing political documents stating that all men are created equally while simultaneously practicing a religious and social order that classified African Americans as second-class citizens.

During my late teens, I felt the same way about Christianity that many of the black Americans who left the faith did. I felt that it was a religion that was imposed upon my ancestors by their slave masters. Around that time, I began to study Islam as a way to free myself from the Eurocentric perspective of Christianity. Islam promoted a sense of brotherhood but it just did not feel like the right home for my soul to be nourished within. I am in no way denigrating Islam. I have friends that practice Islam and they are all wonderful people. The religion just wasn't the right fit for me personally. During my time studying Islam, the spirit of God within me would not allow me to abandon the Christian faith. I knew that I needed to find my place inside the framework of Christianity.

There were three important elements that I discovered that were of utter importance to me finding my place of comfort as a Christian black male. The first element that I discovered is that there truly is power when the name of Jesus is spoken. Every time I would say His name I would feel a sense of peace inside of me.

The second element that I discovered is that the religion of Christianity was practiced in Africa long before the first Africans were enslaved in America. It was practiced in the Kingdom of Axum, which is in the African country of Ethiopia. In the 4th Century AD, Christianity was made the official religion there by the Axumite King Ezana. During this same time period, Christianity was also made the official religion of the Roman Empire by the Emperor Constantine. My discovery of these two important historical developments proved to me that the European slave masters did not introduce Christianity to the African people. The slave masters only force fed their culturally biased Eurocentric perspective of Christianity upon them.

At that point, I was able to free my mind and my spirit away from the Eurocentric perspective of Christianity that I had known for my entire life. I began to see it from an Afrocentric perspective which allowed me to better identify with it as a black male living in America. I also learned about the important roles that Africans played in the Bible. I came to the realization that no group had a monopoly on the religion and that I could comfortably live my life in a manner that I believe is both unashamedly black and unapologetically Christian.

The third important element that led me back to Christianity was my belief in the divinity of Jesus Christ. If you travel to Medina, Saudi Arabia and visit the Al-Masjid al-Nabawi Mosque, you will find the body of the Prophet Muhammad inside of it. If you travel to Jerusalem and visit the Church of Holy Sepulcher, the body of Jesus Christ is not inside of it. There is no denying the fact that the Prophet Muhammad was a powerful messenger, but I could not deny the fact that Jesus was in fact the message.

The apostle John confirms that Jesus was in fact the message in chapter 1 of his account of the gospel. In the gospel of John chapter 1 verses 1-3 it states, "In the beginning was the Word, and the Word was with God, and the Word was God. He was in the beginning with God. All things were made through Him, and without Him nothing was made that was made." John later goes on to affirm the divinity of Jesus by stating, "And the Word became flesh and dwelt among us, and we beheld His glory, the glory as of the only begotten of the Father, full of grace and truth" (John 1:14).

Black Liberation Theology

In the 1960's, there was a great awakening among black Americans, who sought to free themselves from the manacles of race based social oppression. The religion of Christianity was affected by this awakening as well. A new term appeared in the social lexicon called Black Liberation Theology. Dr. James Cone, Dr. Charles Adams, Rev. Jasper Williams and Dr. Jeremiah Wright, among others, became preeminent practitioners in the Black Liberation Theology movement. Current prominent practitioners include: Dr. Frederick D. Haynes III, Dr. William J. Barber II, Bishop Joseph Walker III, Dr. Kevin Cosby, Dr. Jamal Bryant, and Dr. Alyn E. Waller. Notable scholars include: Dr. Cornel West, Dr. Benjamin Chavis, Dr. Obery Hendricks Jr., Dr.

Jawanza Kunjufu and Dr. Michael E. Dyson. This approach to Christianity operates with a Christ like consciousness that seeks to garner social equality and psychological freedom for black Americans and individuals labeled as minorities.

During the 2008 Presidential election, several edited clips of sermons given by then Senator Barack Obama's pastor, Dr. Jeremiah Wright, were widely circulated by the mainstream media. Many black Americans believed that Dr. Wright gave a brutally honest assessment of the plight that black Americans face in our daily navigation in the nation that promotes liberty and justice for all, but displays symptoms of amnesia in its direct correlation to the plight of black Americans. For many white Americans, Wright's sermons were deemed to be unpatriotic and unsettling. His sermon clips also gave them an unfettered livestream glimpse into the other America that mainstream America had largely ignored since the Civil Rights era.

In the 1960's, during the struggle for Civil Rights, black Americans were more unified than at any time during our history within this land. The commonality of our Christian faith helped shape that movement. The black church was the place where we knew the importance of our lives and where our dignity was asserted. It was our safe haven away from oppression and represented the bedrock of our collective unity.

After the assassinations of Malcolm X in 1965, and Dr. Martin Luther King Jr. in 1968, our sense of unity was broken. The flood of drugs into our communities, the lack of emphasis on entrepreneurship and the flight of good paying jobs into suburban communities became a perfect storm leading to the downfall of our communities. Since the 1970's, there has been an advent of single parent homes headed by black mothers, while many black men have become modern day slaves in private, state and federally run correctional facilities. Despite the sustained efforts of

Black Liberation theologians, these developments caused many black Americans to wonder where they fit within the landscape of Christianity. This questioning led to a flight of a great number of black men away from Christianity and into the arms of Islam.

Rewriting Black History

From birth in this country, we are inundated with the tenets of European exceptionalism and besieged with the images of African inferiority. There are so many of you who see the world as I saw it. You see Jesus as I saw Him and you see the white male as I saw him as well. The time has come for us to change the narrative of who Jesus is and what our relation is to Him. It is time to rewrite our history in this land that is called the United States of America. No matter who is in a place of political power, the power to rewrite our own history is in our hands.

In order to accomplish this, we must know our history beyond what the history books taught us in school. We must learn about the dynasties that existed in Africa, generations before Portugal captured the first African slaves in 1441. The success of dynasties such as the Kushite, Axumite, and Keita must be read about and celebrated. These kingdoms possessed great wealth in the form of minerals, livestock and land.

They were not enslaved, but were instead free and creative innovators, who each built thriving empires. Mainstream history books bear no trace of their empires. They will however inform you about slavery, Jim Crow laws and other ways in which African Americans were historical victims. The problem with this rationale is that it presents a distorted view of our true history. It reminds us of our perceived inferiority and does not allow us to know about how successful and prosperous our ancestors once were.

Black America, it is time for us to live our lives in the paint. Life is a lot like the game of basketball. The problem that many of us have is that we believe that the three-point shot is the only way that we can win in life. The three-point shot are the dreams many of us have for financial success in the areas of athletics and entertainment. They are long-shot opportunities with a very low percentage chance for successful achievement. In other words, the space at the top is limited.

Much of what the world sees as the representation and hears as the voice of the black American culture comes from entertainers and athletes. There are millions of African Americans who feel that their voices are not heard or well represented by celebrities from within our culture. When we walk into a bookstore, we have to search very hard to find books that are written from our cultural perspective and often those books are written by athletes or entertainers bereft of scholarship and devoid of intellectual substance. When we turn on the television or listen to the radio, the interviews that we see and hear are often composed of material that typecasts us by the mainstream media stereo that our hands are often restricted from accessing.

I know that many of the athletes and entertainers do the best job that they can to represent our community, but they are not the sole representatives of it. There is a hunger in the African American community to see the linguistic scholarship of writers and to hear the voices of intellectual thinkers that will heighten the spiritual and psychological consciousness of our community. For the vast majority of us, neither athletics nor entertainment will represent our pathway to success.

There are less than 500 NBA players, less than 1700 NFL players and only about 750 professional baseball players. All of these sports have a career expectancy of less than six years. The chances of becoming a world-famous platinum selling recording artist or an A list film star are even less. Just as in basketball, the best way to achieve success is to live your life in the paint. The paint is the business world and a place where the percentages for success are much higher. It is much easier to score shooting a layup or slam dunking as opposed to shooting three-pointers.

The paint is the place where only our education can take us to and where only our faith in God can take us through. The education that we must have goes beyond K-12 or University lecture halls. It encompasses life skills, skills of trade, basic economics and knowledge of self. The paint is a frightening place with many tough obstacles. In basketball, there are flying elbows and hands swatting at you. There are people looking to take a charge or steal the ball from you. In life there is peer pressure, financial struggle and dream thieves in many different forms.

It is strength and confidence in your ability that will help you wield your way through the defense. So many of us fear the contact in the paint that we settle for off balance three-point shots or commit a turnover that often lands us in prisons or graveyards. The beautiful thing about layups and dunks is that when we fight through the contact and make our shot, it offers us the opportunity for a three-point play.

The complete picture of black history allows us the opportunity to know and possess our own truth independent of the narrow picture given by mainstream history books. Mainstream history books tell us that our only contribution to this country was that we built the floor, drew the lines and painted the paint. This incomplete historical assessment has contributed to a multi-generational inferiority complex among black people.

In Africa, we owned the court, made the rules and dominated the paint by scoring at will. We are greater than slavery, greater than Jim Crow, greater than the prison industrial complex and greater than being menial servants on the chessboard of social stratification. We are not only princes and princesses in God's kingdom, but we are descendants of earthly kings and queens from Africa, the birthplace of all civilization.

Black history is much more than 28 days in the month of February and it began generations before the year 1619. It is not a one-sided historical perspective told from the viewpoint of the alleged conquering hero. It is more than what social conditioning has inflicted. It is greater than the inferiority complex that casts a pall over black Americans. Black history is the real truth, the whole truth and nothing but the truth. I encourage you to learn the truth for yourself and I hope that you will encourage the people around you to do the same.

Chapter 5 Questions

1. Do I believe that I was made in God's Image?
   _____
   _____
   _____
   _____

2. Do I believe there is power in the name of Jesus?
   _____
   _____
   _____
   _____

3. Do I feel that my life fits inside the framework of Christianity?
   _____
   _____
   _____
   _____

Chapter 6

Individualism vs Collectivism

Within the world system there are two main theories of economics that are consistently highlighted. The two main theories are capitalism and socialism. Capitalism is seen as the dominant world system that saw tremendous growth as a result of the unpaid labor of enslaved Africans in America. In 1865, the 13th Amendment banned chattel slavery in the United States unless an individual was convicted of a crime. In the years following the passage of this particular amendment, the country's economy shifted away from being primarily based upon farming to being primarily based upon the manufacturing of products. This time period is often referred to as the Industrial Revolution.

The Industrial Revolution was a time period that transformed the economic system of the western world from a capitalistic system based upon agriculture to a capitalistic system based upon industrial products. During this historical period, for many Americans, manufacturing products in factories replaced working on farmland as their primary source of economic sustenance. It was a time period in which the western world experienced tremendous growth in both its population and consumption of natural resources.

In the late nineteenth century, the patronymic names of Rockefeller, Dupont, Carnegie, Morgan, and Vanderbilt were associated with wealth and prestige in the United States of America. These names and the fortunes attached to them came as a result of the benefits of a burgeoning capitalist based economic system during the prosperous decades following the Civil War. Today, the patronymic names Gates, Buffet, Walton and Bezos all hold a similar position in today's social hierarchy as their aforementioned wealthy nineteenth century predecessors. A historically famous opponent of the world system that created these aforementioned names and their vast fortunes was Karl Marx.

Marx believed that capitalism was immoral and was a system that was contrary to human nature. Marx believed that capitalism was the economic system in which the economic elites (ownership class) owned the means of production and the individuals that work for them (working class) must sell their time spent working to the economic elites in order to survive. Marx believed that capitalism suppressed the creative potential of most human beings. He believed that it incorrectly tailored their focus to them desiring to make enough money to own the products that they saw created in their society.

The basic tenet of Marx's argument against capitalism is that he believed that people needed to have the freedom to maximize their full potential as human beings. Marx advocated for communism (socialism) in which he believed the power structure that contributed to the unnatural state of human nature would be replaced, and that people would be allowed to live their lives in a way that maximized their potential. Marx envisioned a utopian world society that placed each individual worker on the same economic level. Today, in our capitalistic society, to be labeled a Marxist or a Socialist is akin to being given a scarlet letter.

Capitalism is seen as a system that is squarely on the ideological side of individualism, while collectivism and its concepts, in relation to economics, are seen as being more in line with a socialist perspective. I believe that both capitalism and socialism have good and bad components within their structures. Since the United States is a capitalist country, it is the system that black Americans must learn to find our success within.

Each year Forbes magazine profiles the 400 richest Americans inside of its pages. These 400 individuals are touted as winners within the capitalistic system which prides itself upon individualistic principles. Does this mean that the more than 300 million other Americans who fail to make the cut are losers? I do not believe that it does in the least bit. The individualist would say that success is the result of our own efforts, while collectivists would retort that success is a team effort of individuals working to help one another succeed. In the United States, we can see the divide between the individualist and collectivist mindset in the two main political parties within our country.

Republicans and their individualist mindsets often speak about cutting socially based programs and freeing the economy from government regulations. They often speak of being on the side of business and for cutting taxes on people they term as job creators. They also are often heard talking about the role of an individual in relation to the success of a society.

Democrats and their collectivist mindsets speak about pouring money into social programs and increasing taxes and regulations on businesses in an effort to level the economic playing field to benefit the poor and middle class. They often speak about the role of society in relation to the success of an individual. The politically divided mindsets featuring rank individualism and class collectivism have also been woven into the cultural methodologies adopted by organizations.

The US Presidential election, in the year 2016, could have potentially featured the United States deciding to elect individualist minded businessman Donald Trump, versus a collectivist minded Senator from Vermont named Bernie Sanders. If I had my choice between the two I would align myself with Sanders and his collectivist approach. I believe that each of us on this earth is not responsible for just ourselves but for the well-being of our fellow humans around us as well. Some people may need an economic hand up in order to help them rise out of the rungs of poverty and into the ranks of the middle class. I would much rather see my tax dollars go towards assisting individuals in need rather than to bomb nations that most Americans could hardly point to on a globe.

I believe that my collectivist mindset is rooted in my interpretation of Christianity. I am a Christian and consider myself to be an ardent follower of the teachings of Jesus Christ. The Jesus figure that I read about came to serve His fellow man as opposed to being served by them. In the biblical gospel of Mark, Jesus states, "For even the Son of Man did not come to be served, but to serve, and to give His life a ransom for many" (Mark 10:45). From my reading, I interpret Jesus to be much more of a collectivist than an individualist. I don't believe that He would agree that the achievement of His own happiness was His highest moral purpose, as Ayn Rand believed it should be for humans. It appears to me that He believed that serving others was more important than being served by others.

The Forbes List and Black America

Each year since 2004, I have made it a point of

personal emphasis to read through the Forbes 400 list. I peruse through it annually to see which individuals occupy the top positions on the economic food chain in the United States. I particularly look at which companies they own and how those companies are performing.

In 2017, the lowest ranked individual on the list had a net worth of 2 billion dollars and the highest ranked person was Microsoft founder Bill Gates whose net worth was listed at approximately 89 billion dollars. President Donald Trump was ranked at number 248 on the list with a net worth of 3.1 billion dollars. Out of 400 people on the list there were only two black Americans listed. Media mogul Oprah Winfrey was ranked at number 264 with a net worth of 3 billion dollars and private equity CEO Robert Smith was ranked at number 226 with a net worth of 3.3 billion dollars.

In my estimation, there is room for at least twelve more black Americans on the Forbes 400 list with Oprah Winfrey and Robert Smith, based upon our percentage of the United States population. I believe that it will take a collectivist minded approach to the economic system of capitalism in order to make this a reality. Black Americans must learn to capitalize within the system of capitalism. We should not seek to gain all of our opportunities for success from others when we possess the individual and collective strength to create our own. We have the power to live our lives by our own system of design and not by someone else's created system of default. Money is generated from providing a meaningful service. Large amounts of it are generated when meaningful service becomes a brand with a loyal consumer base.

It is no secret that the wealth rankings in this country are dominated by European Americans. The Forbes 400 list is empirical evidence of that fact. We cannot depend upon the wealth that lies in their hands to create the opportunities that will improve the fortunes of black Americans. We must seek to create both our individual wealth and the opportunities that will benefit the collective. You may never become a billionaire and make the Forbes 400 list. You may never even become a millionaire. Despite that you have within your hands the ability to be the best person that you can be. You have a responsibility to determine God's purpose for your life and live it.

In the 1950's and 60's our sense of collective unity forced the integration of school buildings, corporations, political offices and shopping districts. There was one thing that we failed to integrate as a collective and that is the dollar. In the 2010's and 20's we must work in concert to integrate the dollar. Dr. Martin Luther King Jr. led the fight for Civil Rights. The fight for Silver Rights will be led by the person in the mirror.

Christ Influenced Social Humanism

In his August 1967 speech to the Southern Christian Leadership Conference titled, *Where Do We Go From Here*, Dr. King provided his personal assessment of both capitalism and communism. He stated, "What I'm saying to you this morning is communism forgets that life is individual. Capitalism forgets that life is social. And the kingdom of brotherhood is found neither in the thesis of communism nor the antithesis of capitalism, but in a higher synthesis. It is found in a higher synthesis that combines the truth of both. Now when I say questioning the whole society, it means ultimately coming to see that the problem of racism, the problem of economic exploitation, and the problem of war are all tied together."

Dr. King firmly understood that in order for black Americans to have success in this world, it was imperative that we learned to function within the global economic system of capitalism. He desired for us to find success, in the same global system that had successfully exploited the unpaid labor of Africans in the Americas. It was the unbridled spirit of capitalism that caused our ancestors to be forcibly removed from their homeland and placed into involuntary servitude. The usage of their free labor made the United States and several European countries into economic superpowers. The descendants of those slaves will most likely never be paid reparations for the economic castration and psychological emasculation that was done to our ancestors.

Individuals that are totally consumed by the spirit of capitalism love the fruits of it (money) and often obtain it by using methods that may cause harm to others. In my estimation, there is nothing wrong with desiring to have an abundance of money. I do not begrudge anyone for wanting to make a lot of money. My issue is with those individuals who do it in a ruthless manner with a reckless disregard for the well-being of God's children.

It will take a concentrated collectivist approach by black Americans committed to earnestly working within the system of capitalism to create our own remedy to the systematic oppression of economic inequality. Our success in capitalism must be guided by the spirit of God and not by the spirit of capitalism. I believe that there is a concept that can allow a person to be successful in capitalism and successfully operate with the heart of God's spirit.

The concept is called Christ Influenced Social-Humanism. This concept encourages us to see our fellow human beings as children of God and not as means of exploitation. It is essentially capitalism with a conscience. It is a success based mindset that encompasses a wealth consciousness that features a concern for the betterment of the collective world society. I believe that it represents the higher synthesis that will combine the truth of both capitalism and communism in an effective manner. It also represents the practical social application of the principles of Black Liberation Theology.

Life is not about how many impressive deals you can close. When your life is over, the number of lives you touch will mean much more than the number reflected on your bank statement. Your legacy is what you create. God will give you the tools but you are the contractor in charge of constructing the masterpiece. You can make the choice to either be a product of your environment or make your environment a product of you.

Thermometer vs Thermostat

I have learned in my lifetime that some individuals are thermometer people and others are thermostat people. Thermometer people are individuals that go along to get along. Many of them complain about their circumstances or view injustices but never take actions towards changing their environments. In contrast, thermostat people are the individuals that change the atmosphere wherever they go. They are the influential individuals that seek to better the circumstances of those around them. When others may cower due to their fears and shrink in the face of injustice, thermostat people try to change their circumstances to specifically reflect how they desire them to be. These are the individuals who are willing to make sacrifices in order to facilitate the success of the collective. They are the individuals who make the consistent choice to choose faith over fear.

Are you a thermometer or a thermostat? Are you an individual that complains about your circumstances or do you strive to make improvements? Thermometer people are powerless to make changes because their thoughts imprison them behind the stone walls of ambition. The only thing that separates thermometer people from thermostat people is their ability to believe in themselves and their intrinsic belief that they are worthy of excellence.

Being a thermostat person is what each of us should strive to become. There are more than enough thermometer people in this world. There is a dire need for many more thermostats. Each of us gets one chance to live on this earth. That one chance that we are blessed with must be maximized. Being a thermometer type of person will not maximize it. Making up your mind to be a thermostat type of person will not only maximize your own potential, but it could potentially change the world.

Chapter 6 Questions

1. Do I identify myself as an individualist or as a collectivist?

2. Do I know how to be successful in the system of capitalism?

3. Am I a thermometer or a thermostat type of individual?

PART TWO

THROUGH THE WILDERNESS

Chapter 7

Survival to Success

In order to achieve any goal whether it is a group goal or an individual goal it requires the combination of discipline and persistence. In his bestselling book, titled *Think and Grow Rich*, Napoleon Hill extolled the virtues of being persistent and having a definitive purpose. There are so many people walking the earth that are clueless as to what they want to specifically accomplish with their life. When a person is disciplined they often remain focused on accomplishing any task that is placed in front of them. A disciplined person is willing to make sacrifices in order to reach their goal. The thought of succeeding drives them to achieve their goal beyond the obstacles that may come in their path.

In our world today there are distractions all around us. A benefit of modern technology is the convenience that it brings to our everyday lives. A major drawback of it is the distractions that it brings about as well. For millions of people the inability to employ self-discipline is the chief element preventing them from living their lives to the level that God created them to reach. This is often a source of frustration for many people who struggle daily with the reality of living their lives with unfulfilled dreams. In my life, I have learned that hard work and regret both cause pain but only one of them can produce lasting rewards.

I was told when I was growing up, that I would have to work twice as hard as the people around me in order to succeed in this country. The social, economic, political and religious climates in this country are shaped by Eurocentric viewpoints which are cloaked in an unquestioned aura of patrilineality. In my lifetime, I do not expect this to change. The election of Donald Trump to the office of President is another notch in the garment belt of white male privilege. It also represents the political offspring of the benefits of celebrity status and wealth.

The deafening cries by many conservatives since the 2008 Presidential election, to take their alleged country back and to Make America Great Again, have been thinly veiled attempts to undermine the rise of non-European Americans into positions of economic and political power. They are acts that prey on the fears of those individuals who have lived throughout their entire lives with the belief that European American economic and political domination is a permanent status quo and not a calculated method of operation in the United States of America.

Black Americans work very hard in this country to make a living just as people from other ethnic groups do. We also seemingly work just as hard to try to gain social acceptance from many people who do not see us as their economic, political or religious equal. We seemingly only matter to conservatives as long as we can entertain them or make them money. We seemingly only matter to liberals when they desire our unwavering support to keep them entrenched in positions of power. We also only seemingly matter to them as long as we can entertain them or make them money.

Conservatives treat us field slaves and liberals treat us as house servants. The Republican Party treats us as if we are starving peasants deemed worthy of eating discarded scraps from the trash can of second-class citizenship. The Democratic Party treats us as if we are crumb snatching children deemed incapable of preparing our own meals inside of the kitchen of prosperity. Neither of the major political parties displays an overwhelming desire to see us economically prosperous or politically powerful.

Breaking The Chains

You are responsible for your own freedom in this land. In the 21st century your freedom is based upon your ability to create wealth for yourself and those around you. Post traumatic slave syndrome has conditioned blacks in this country to find their sense of happiness by building the dreams of someone else while neglecting to employ the necessary level of self-discipline to build their own. It has also conditioned the minds of a great number of younger African Americans into consistently allowing the opinions of entertainers to carry more weight than the researched antidotes of information unearthed by our scholars.

African Americans have-allowed this conditioning- due to the commandeering of our media perceptions by individuals that do not share our ancestral DNA; nor do they share an equitable share in the common stock of our cultural progression. For several generations, they have reaped economic dividends by directly profiting from our misery. Their commandeering is a direct result of our lack of ownership stakes in the economic and political arenas of this country.

There are millions of black Americans who wake up every day and face the harsh reality of living in the United

States of America and being perceived as second-class citizens. They face this life without the beneficial shields of tangible wealth or celebrity status. The daily plight of black Americans is not an easy one. The well documented issues in black American society today are not present because we don't believe that we can succeed in this country. They are present because we have been culturally conditioned to see survival as success and achievement as a wish only granted by the genie of circumstance. In our effort to survive in this country, we have often sacrificed substance and settled for symbolism in relation to our progress.

We expect to survive and are surprised when we succeed. This mentality must be changed if we are to live our lives to the maximum capacity that God created for us to live. We must expect to be successful and create our own blueprint to become successful. The evils of false European supremacy conditioned us for survival in this country but our God created us for success here. Your life will either represent a function of your condition or a true reflection of our God.

Any place that we go to in life, our thoughts lead us there before our physical bodies arrive there. I discussed earlier in this book the power of imagery as it relates to the commonly seen historical artist renditions of Jesus Christ. Thoughts truly do become things. Everything that you can see in this world first began as a thought in the mind of someone. If a person has a mindset that focuses upon finding ways to survive, they will act in a manner that displays a survival based mindset. If a person has a mindset that focuses upon finding ways to succeed, they will act in a manner that displays a success based mindset.

There is no denying the fact that black Americans are very strong people. Our ancestors survived the harrowing middle passage from Africa and several generations of enslavement. We along with our parents and grandparents have survived the last 153 years, which have featured the struggle to obtain the basic rights that the Declaration of Independence and the United States Constitution speak of. The common theme through all of it has been our focus on survival.

For nearly 400 years, survival is what we have been known for in this country. The hour has now come for our focus to change. Our mindset must now become one that focuses upon success. Our focus on success must be done in the face of discrimination, in the face of unfavorable media perception and done in the face of our challenges to acquire wealth building capital. The survival mindset is what our history in this country is built upon but the success mindset must become what our future is based upon.

If you look at immigrants that come to this country from other nations, there is a common theme that many of them share. Their commonality is found inside the common thread of their desire to succeed. Some of them are unable to speak the English language when they arrive here, but they carry determination within their spirits. Our faith in God is the key that will open the gate to any blessing that God desires for us.

This is the only life that you have and there is nothing that you can do about the color of your skin. It is the way that God made you. There is little that you can do if someone is prejudiced towards your skin color without examining the content of your heart. What you can do is believe that God loves you and that He created each of His children in His image.

Each person on earth is painted with the colors of God's love. When Jesus came to earth, He did not come here to simply survive. He came to earth to succeed with His God ordained mission to give the gift of eternal salvation. Despite the obstacles that He faced, He never lost focus on the mission that He was sent to complete. God did not send any of us to earth to save the world as He did with

Jesus. We were each sent here to represent Him and carry out specific assignments during our lives on this earth.

True success is manifested with the combination of faith and love. Survival is manifested due to fear and an acute lack of knowledge. I understand there will be days when we will feel as if we are surviving and not succeeding. Even in those times it is critical that we continue to maintain a success based mindset.

A survival based mindset suppresses the ability of individuals to critically think. This mindset has led to the fear of success and faith in disappointment that keeps the divine purpose of millions of people at bay. You must believe that you deserve to prosper and that you are capable of experiencing success in every area of your life. You must firmly believe in your mind that the weight of your potential can consistently break the scale of your circumstances. Your knowledge of this will keep your mind strong during times when success seems to be elusive.

Taking Our Culture Back

I believe there is a symbiotic relationship between artistry and the culture that births it. In our current society today, some people wonder if artistry has a greater influence on culture or if culture has a greater influence on artistry. I am of the belief that the influence that artistry places upon a culture is a direct reflection of the value that the culture itself assigns to the artists and their artistic interpretations. I believe that for black Americans, our culture assigns a very high social value to the artistry that is birthed from it.

In the early 1990's, gangsta rap, which often glorified violence and the disrespect of black women began to dominate the airwaves. The lyrics that the artists used were based upon what they grew up seeing in the environments that they were raised in. Their music indirectly became the soundtrack for black American life and became the vivid description of our plight.

Gangsta rap has generated billions of dollars in profits over the last several decades. It has played a major role in shaping the self-concept of a large number of young black Americans. It has served them intellectual gruel over hot beats that have enticed them into subconsciously sacrificing the sanctity of their souls beneath the idol of abject materialism. Much of the music contains lyrics that promote violence, drug usage and hypersexuality. This has contributed to the decay of both our collective self-esteem and moral fiber. It has also represented the reflection of a survival based mindset.

Black Americans are not gangsta's, we are royalty. Our music should reflect where we desire to go in life as opposed to where we have been. In the Presidential era of Donald Trump, and beyond, our desire for success as a people must become paramount. Artists have platforms that are able to influence the minds and decisions of millions of people. It is not their job to be role models, but I would like to challenge them to be responsible with the content of their lyrics.

I believe that the artistry of black Americans should reflect love and liberation. It should also feature a wealth based consciousness that inspires us to operate our lives from the apex of our intelligence. In our current state, our community is out of balance with the essence of who we truly are. I believe that the quality of our artistry has the power to improve both the nature of our culture and restore the proper essence of who we are as a community. It should reflect the advancement of the cognitive maturation of our thoughts. We must seek to regain control of our art and the themes of our messages from cultural vultures that care more about profit margins than improving the societal landscape for African Americans.

In the 1960's, the music of black Americans was shaped by our struggle for economic equality and social equity. The music contained themes that made us see ourselves as a unified community. Back then, many of the record labels were black owned entities that believed in enlightenment as well as entertainment. These labels such as Motown, Stax and Philadelphia International were pivotal in shaping the collective consciousness of black Americans. Over the last several decades, black Americans have lost creative control of our art due to the desires of corporations that have profited greatly by highlighting the negative aspects of our community.

We possess the ability to regain control of our art through the usage of our dollars. In order to increase the volume of our God consciousness, our artistry must find the synchronistic balance between the treble of economic sustenance and the bass of social responsibility. If we make collective decisions to support artistry that portrays us in a positive light, it will challenge the creativity of our artists to match the desires of our tastes. It will also force the executives that oversee the production of our artists to either seek to profit from the content of our intelligence or to seek their profits away from our community altogether. I understand that this transition will not happen overnight, but I believe that we can begin to change things starting today.

African American scholar, Dr. Boyce Watkins once stated, "If you teach intelligence, thousands will listen. If you preach ignorance, you'll have an audience of millions." In order for African Americans to exit the wilderness of our oppression, intelligence must have an audience of millions and ignorance must have an audience of few. We must regain ownership and control the production of what we create. For some of us, in our effort to survive, ignorance has been a place of bliss, but for all of us to succeed, intelligence must become our place of inhabitance.

Taking Authority

    I firmly believe that knowing your value is the key to living a purpose driven life in a money driven world. In order to know your value, you must live your life with the knowledge that God loves you unconditionally. You are one of His children. Until a person knows that God loves them unconditionally, it is impossible for them to love their own self unconditionally. When a person is unable to love their own self unconditionally, it is impossible for them to love others unconditionally.

    Ultimately, God is the representation of unconditional love. Unconditional love is the kind of love that is given without expectations or requirements. When we choose to love ourselves unconditionally and earnestly seek to love others unconditionally, we are able to best represent God on this earth. In order to walk in the full authority of God's purpose for your life, you must learn to operate with the spirit of His unconditional love.

    No matter what situation you were born into, or the circumstances that you are currently facing, God created your life to fulfill a unique purpose. In the book of Jeremiah, it states, "Before I formed you in the womb I knew you" (Jeremiah 1:5). This verse serves as a reminder to us that our lives on this earth are not accidental occurrences. Each of us was meant to inhabit the earth at the exact time that God ordained for our lives. God, in His divine providence, did not send you to this earth to suffer more than you succeed. Further into the book of Jeremiah it states, "For I know the thoughts that I think toward you, says the Lord, thoughts of peace and not of evil, to give you a future and a hope" (Jeremiah 29:11).

    I am aware in our society today of the popular colloquialism, "our circumstances dictate our actions." I believe that as children of God, empowered by the Holy Spirit, we have the power to dictate our actions towards our circumstances. You were not created by God to live on this earth as a perpetual victim of circumstances. You were sent to this earth to circumvent circumstances and to succeed by fulfilling the unique purpose that God created for you to achieve.

The Spirit

The spirit of God will give us the tools that we need to succeed in life. In order to hear from God, it is important to pray and create a space for God to enter into your life. God often speaks to us in a whisper. The whisper, or still small voice as some like to call it, is most audible when we are quiet. Just prior to His crucifixion, Jesus spoke to His disciples about the coming of the Holy Spirit.

In the book of John chapter 14 verse 15-17 He states, "If you love me, keep My commandments, and I will pray the Father, and He will give you another Helper, that He may abide with you forever the Spirit of truth, whom the world cannot receive, because it neither sees Him nor knows Him; but you know Him, for He dwells with you and will be in you." Allow the power of the Spirit of truth that Jesus spoke about to guide you daily. I implore you to walk in the power of that Spirit and the seemingly impossible will become your future reality.

The Divine Purpose of Your Gift

You may never become a world-famous celebrity for using your gift. Your gifts and talents may prove to be most impactful to the people around you. The world media may not know your name but God does. He sees the positive impact that you have on the people around you. He celebrates your life, and He created you to be successful. It is imperative that you see yourself how God sees you.

You are the role model for someone around you. They may not know anyone that is a world-famous celebrity, but they know you and they see how you choose to live your life. These people are often represented in the form of our family members, friends, co-workers and people that we encounter while participating in our daily activities. The people in our society that we view as celebrities are normal people with exceptional talent. Whether they are athletes, entertainers or even preachers, God created each of them in the same manner that He created you. They were able to develop their talent to a level that allows it to be showcased to the world. There is nothing wrong with appreciating their talents, but they are not idols to be worshipped.

In our world today, we are inundated with the images of alleged reality television. These shows have executive producers that are well-paid to create cinematic narratives that produce entertainment value and generate viewer interest. There are billion-dollar industries that are built to capitalize upon the benefits of us minding someone else's personal business. Daily we digest digital images that feature the poisoned apples of other people's insecurities and vanity. There is no need to wonder why we are often hampered from ingesting the fruits of our own success.

People are created by God to be appreciated but not idolized. There are media entities that attempt to program our minds to value the opinions of people who often do not know who they truly are as individuals outside of their occupations or financial net worth. The media entities do this because they fully understand that it is easy to generate consistently large profits from the habits and actions of a manipulated mind.

In terms of celebrities, we know their talents but we do not know them personally or the struggles they face as human beings. The world that we live in currently, seems to value social media likes more than it seems to value impactful content. This world does an incredible job of building people up and desiring to see them fall after they have achieved a modicum of success. This world is a commercialized space in which we are conditioned by our society to believe that as long as someone makes money, they must be doing things the right way. This incorrect assessment has caused millions of people to value the counterfeit living of ratchetness over seeking to live the reality of a righteous life.

With my words, I am not seeking to condemn anyone. I am seeking to simply point out the stark contrasts between living a life that pleases God versus one that pleases the world. As believers in God, we live in this world but are not made of this world. We are children of God who possess His spirit. The gospel of John records the final prayer that Jesus made to God in reference to His disciples. He stated to God, "I have given them Your word; and the world has hated them because they are not of the world, just as I am not of the world. I do not pray that You should take them out of the world, but that You should keep them from the evil one. They are not of the world, just as I am not of the world. Sanctify them by Your truth. Your word is truth. As You sent Me into the world, I also have sent them into the world" (John 17: 14-18).

A lifetime of positive impact on others means much more than the fifteen minutes of fame that some desire to attain. The prostitution of your values and the destruction of your moral compass are not worth someone else's unladen opinion of your life. A successful life is built with high levels of character and high levels of integrity. These are the fraternal twins birthed from the authenticity of self. They represent the fixed social adhesive that sustains the achievement of success over time. Our lives are always evolving and will always be under construction by God. The solid foundation for our success must incorporate the materials of high character and high integrity.

To transition from a life of constant survival to one of God favored success, you must know yourself and you must be true to the reality of who you are. For some of us, this transition may be a difficult task to undertake. Please know that God is always in control and that your success matters to Him. This world may have conditioned you for survival, but God created you for success. He sent you into the world to obtain it and with His power you will achieve it.

Whenever my phone rings there is often someone on the other end of it calling me for encouragement. From birth God blessed me with the innate ability to encourage others. Encouraging others comes natural to me and it is what I love to do. It is my unique gift from God. My unique gift equips me with the ability to effectively communicate with others. As I worked to develop my gift over time, I discovered that my ability to effectively communicate with others is best transmuted into the talents of inspirational writing and motivational speaking. Through the application of my writing and speaking talents, I am blessed to be able to inspire and encourage the people that God places in my path.

When I was nineteen years old, I set a goal to become the best inspirational writer and motivational speaker in the world. At that time, I believed the measurement of my level of success would be best reflected in how much money I would eventually make as a result of the application of my talents. In the years since then, I have grown closer in my walk with God through prayer and meditation.

Over time as my spiritual vibration and level of God consciousness elevated, I reached the realization that my previous measurement of success was incorrect. I learned that the positive difference in the number of lives that my talents impacted was of greater importance than the amount of money that I made from them. As believers in God, our success on this earth is tied to our willingness to obey the instructions that we receive from the Holy Spirit. In my own life, the I AM power of the Holy Spirit has provided for me the ideas that have been essential to my success. The Holy Spirit has also been instrumental in helping me to determine exactly who needs to experience the application of my gifts and talents and exactly when they need to experience them.

In the black community, there is a fascination that many of us have with playing the numbers. Many of us dream about someday selecting the right lottery numbers and winning instant access to life changing wealth. The odds of winning a Mega Millions jackpot are 1 in 258,890,850. The odds of winning a Powerball jackpot are a little bit tougher at 1 in 292,201,338. In contrary, I have learned that the odds of having a successful life by combining your gifts and talents with the power of the Holy Spirit are much higher at 1 in 1. The odds of winning the lottery sponsored by your faith, which is heaven sent, are much higher than winning the one sponsored by your state of residence.

When your phone rings, what do people call you in search of? What is the unique talent that you have that may be a struggle for someone else but comes natural to you? Your answers to those two aforementioned questions are the clues that will assist you in uncovering God's purpose for your life. The people that are around you need to experience the application of your gifts and talents. You are the person that God has placed in their path, and He is counting on you to display His reflection through the application of your gifts and talents.

The most important measurement of your success is not found within dollars and cents. Your success is best measured in the positive difference that you make in the lives of others. In his letter to the church at Philippi the Apostle Paul wrote, "And my God shall supply all your needs according to His riches in glory by Christ Jesus" (Philippians 4:19).

I encourage you to live your life with the knowledge that God will supply all of your needs. When you seek to bless and enrich the lives of others, God will touch the hearts of others to ultimately bless and enrich your own life. The jackpot of blessings that you need will not be found in a nightly drawing but it will instead be given to you through your daily prayer. Your faith is the ticket that you will need to transition your life from simply surviving the odds to successfully beating them.

Chapter 7 Questions

1. Do I have a survival or a success mentality?

2. What does a success mentality resemble to me?

3. Do I believe the responsibility for my success is in my own hands?

Chapter 8

Playing The Trump Card

In a game of cards trump cards are the cards that are ranked above all the other cards. They are cards that can guarantee victory for the player when played correctly. Our faith in God serves as our trump card in this life. In life, I believe that a relationship with God is essential to any success that a person may have. In order for us to make our relationship with God a success it requires us to place our faith in Him. The book of Hebrews chapter 11 verse 1 states, "Now faith is the substance of things hoped for, the evidence of things not seen."

There is no question that the after effects of slavery have given European Americans an advantage to economic success in this country. As I mentioned earlier in this book, black Americans were not born into a level playing field here. There is something special that does however provide each of us with the opportunity to level the playing field. That something special is the element of faith.

God loves all of His children equally. No person created by God is inherently better or worse than anyone else. What separates us as people are the frequency levels of our spiritual vibrations and the decisions that we make as a result of our knowledge of it. Our successes and failures in life often result from the decisions that we make with the options that are attracted to us. As our decision making improves, our options often improve as well. Living a life of faith and listening to the spirit of God will compel you to make the best decisions for your life.

There are days and for that matter seasons in our lives that will bring about times of uncertainty. It is important to recognize that the faith that we build when times are more certain is the same faith that will sustain us during the times of uncertainty. The concept is similar to how an athlete trains during the off season of their particular sport.

The off-season training prepares the athletes minds, spirits and bodies for whatever elements they may face during the season of their sport. If the athlete waited until their season started to train for their season, they would put themselves at risk for injury and most likely would not perform to the best of their abilities. For an athlete off season training often includes weight lifting, running and film study. Elite level athletes often have coaches that assist them with their off season training. Some even train with other athletes as a way to bond and improve their skills.

As believers in God, our off season training also helps us to prepare our minds, spirits and bodies for whatever elements we may face in the challenging seasons of life. If the believer waits until their challenging season of life is upon them, it will potentially place them at risk for taking the ungodly prescriptions of fear as opposed to ingesting the proper solutions of faith. For believers off season training consists of prayer, meditation, study of sacred texts and communal fellowship with other believers. Just as athletes have coaches to assist them, believers have men and women of God known as clergy to fulfill that role.

Facing Tests

There will be days in your life in which faith is all that you will have in your possession. There will be times in life when bad things will happen to good people. There will be times when job losses will occur. There will be times when loved ones will pass away. There will be times when relationships will dissolve. There will even be times when storms will appear out of thin air. What we do in these times is critical. It is easy to lie in bed with the curtains drawn or to drink until we pass out. These actions are temporary measures that may numb our pain, but in my estimation, they do not represent God's best solutions for our lives.

When storms appear, we must seek God's face and infinite wisdom. No one will go through this life immune from the affliction of painful situations. There are times in life when we have to play through our pain in the same manner that athletes do. When a storm comes into our lives it is a time of testing.

Sometimes during our period of testing, God will appear to become silent. This is similar to how teachers are during tests in school. When the teacher hands out a test to his or her students, they expect the student to be prepared to face whatever questions that may be found on their papers. This is due to the teacher preparing the student for the test during the time preceding it. In life when we seek God when things are going well, it helps to prepare us for the storms of life. When the storms hit and we pass through them, it clears the way for us to be promoted by God.

There is someone reading this that may be facing a storm and may not see a way of escape. You may feel as if you are looking into a funnel cloud of uncertainty with peace seeming to be nonexistent. Oftentimes when a storm hits there is no safe place to hide or escape to. The storms in this life must be endured until they pass away from us. Our faith and trust in God serves as our shelter from the storm. Storms will not last. They are only temporary occurrences. I have learned that the blessings that we have long prayed for are oftentimes found on the other side of our place of brokenness. Yes, storms often destroy things and cause damage. Yes, they do invoke thoughts of fear and panic.

In the midst of your storm do not let thoughts that promote fear and discouragement become your guides. Choose to employ faith and confidence instead. You will get through your storm and into the place of your blessing. The key is to keep moving forward and seeking God's wisdom to guide the order of your steps. Yes, it is true that bad things do happen to good people, but I am convinced that passing through the storms of life is what qualifies the good to become great. Do you dare to be great?

Every good thing that I have accomplished in my life came as a result of my choosing faith over fear and belief over doubt. I am a living witness to the power of positive thinking and speaking. The same energy that it takes to be fearful is the same amount that it takes to live faith filled. You are a refined child of God and not a situation that someone else defines. If you have the vision, our Father in heaven has the provision to meet your needs.

See each day as a new opportunity to feed your faith and starve your fears. God has created you to do great things during your time on this earth. It is time to put your faith into action and believe that there is truly nothing too hard for the power of God to manifest in your life.

Fear and Doubt

I know that you have dreams inside of you. You can visualize yourself living them out but something inside of you keeps holding you back from believing that your vision will become a reality. There are two variables that most people have in common that prevent their dreams from exiting their imaginations. The two variables are fear and doubt. They are the dream predators that have snuffed out the dreams of millions of people.

Fear and doubt manifest from internal thoughts of inferiority and perceived weakness. They are also spawned from the negative words of other people. A reason that prevents many people from succeeding in life is they allow the fear filtered watering of other people's opinions to extinguish the flames of their own faith. You must know that God has not given you a spirit of fear. In the book of 2nd Timothy chapter 1 verse 7 it states "For God has not given us a spirit of fear, but of power and of love and of a sound mind."

Our God does not operate in response to fear and doubt. He operates as a result of faith and belief. The world conditions us to operate in fear and doubt but for God's people this is an unacceptable way to live. In the book of Romans chapter 12 verse 2 the Apostle Paul writes, "And do not be conformed to this world, but be transformed by the renewing of your mind, that you may prove what is that good and acceptable and perfect will of God."

This basically says that we are born into this world but are not creations of it. We were created by God in heaven and sent to live here. God has tailor made your being and created an assignment that only you can carry out on this earth. Your life has a divine purpose and destiny attached to it. The only way that you can execute your assignment is through the power of faith and belief.

I know that there will be times in life when fear and doubt will invade your mind. Do not speak aloud their prescriptions for your life. You must tune them out and speak words of faith and believe within your spirit and mind what you are declaring over your life. There is a God power within you that is stronger than any negative force that you will face on this earth. You will accomplish your dreams and turn your vision into a reality. All you must do is ignite your faith and begin to move your mind and body in the direction of your dreams. The ungodly spirits of fear and doubt are no match against God inspired faith and belief.

In the United States of America there has been a culture of fear following September 11th 2001. This has been a specific fear of terrorists potentially seeking to harm our country. When President Barack Obama won the 2008 Presidential election, there were fears among conservatives that he would promote a radical agenda that would cause irreparable harm to the country. Their fears were never realized. When President Trump won the 2016 Presidential election, the same fears that conservatives previously felt about President Obama were then felt by liberals. Their fears will hopefully not be realized either.

Fear is man's greatest tool to both distract and manipulate the minds of a population. It is promoted by media entities and it divides God's people. It also blocks the blessings of God due to our faith being inactivate while our fear is active. Are you a person of faith or a person of fear? If the passage in second Timothy is correct, then we must understand that the God we serve does not promote fear. He is a God of faith and those of us who serve Him are people of faith. Fear has the power to paralyze your life while faith has the power to promote it to greater levels. It is essential that you choose the benefits of promotion over the deficits of stagnation. The level of your faith has the power to raise the quality of your life to reach staggering heights of achievement.

Miracle of Faith

Found within the gospel account of Matthew there is an important illustration concerning the power of faith and the power of fear and doubt. The disciples were out fishing one night when they saw a man walking on the sea. They believed that they were seeing a ghost but it was in fact Jesus who was walking on the sea. In Matthew chapter 14 verse 28, His chief Apostle Peter says, "Lord, if it is You, command me to come to You on the water." Jesus then commanded Peter to come to Him and he began to walk on the water toward Jesus. But when he saw that the wind was boisterous; he was afraid; and beginning to sink he cried out, saying, "Lord save me!" And immediately Jesus stretched out His hand and caught him, and said to him, "O you of little faith, why did you doubt?" (Matthew 14:28-31)

Peter was able to perform the same miracle of walking on water that he had just watched Jesus do. He accomplished it when he was filled with faith and kept his eye on Jesus. Even though the storm was raging around him, he was safe during the entire time that he kept his focus on Jesus. When feelings of fear and doubt caused him to turn his attention towards the power of the blowing winds and took his focus away from Jesus, he began to fall beneath the water which he had previously walked above.

As you read this book, you are probably sitting down in a chair or on a couch. You have enough faith to believe that what you are sitting on will hold you up and keep you from falling. If you did not possess that faith you would most likely not feel safe sitting where you currently are. If you can have faith that a chair or couch that a person made will hold you up and keep you from falling; how can you ever doubt the power of the God that created you? Our safety comes from placing our faith in Him. You must believe in your heart that He will hold you up and keep you from falling.

Peter walked on water for the exact amount of time that he believed that he could. His faith was the substance that created the miracle that matched the same one that Jesus was simultaneously performing. In order for Peter to perform the miracle of walking on the water, the only prerequisite that he needed was faith. Jesus did not ask him about the color of his skin. He did not ask him about his political affiliation. The neighborhood he grew up in did not matter either. All that mattered was his level of faith.

In the Old Testament, when the prophet Samuel was sent by God to find King David, God gave him specific instructions. "Do not look at his appearance or at his physical stature, because I have refused him. For the Lord does not see as man sees; for man looks at outward appearance, but the Lord looks at the heart" (1 Samuel 16:7). If God looked at your heart today would He see faith living inside of it or would He see it filled with fear? My prayer is that you choose the pathway of faith and become all that God created you to be. Your fear has the power to destroy your dreams. Your faith has the power to create your miracles. This is your trump card in life. It is God's gift to you and it is your responsibility to play it.

Chapter 8 Questions

1. Do I believe that my faith is my trump card?
   _____
   _____
   _____
   _____

2. Is my level of faith stronger than my level of fear?
   _____
   _____
   _____
   _____

3. Do I believe that my faith can produce miracles?
   _____
   _____
   _____
   _____

Chapter 9

Applied Faith

Faith is what my life is built upon. Faith represents the currency of blessings and it is what attracts the undivided attention of God to our needs. It is the call that God responds to when He chooses to send favor in our direction. It is through faith that we are able to speak things that are not as though they were. Faith fills our minds with determined thoughts. On the contrary, fear fills our minds with desperate ones. Each decision that we make in our life is based upon either faith or fear.

A great number of the systems that comprise the world that we live in are empowered by a culture of fear. Whether it is in corporations, government entities or even religious denominations, they all exercise their power based upon fear. In our modern world, faith is often relegated to a position that is out of sight and out of mind. In order to reach the destiny that God has for our lives, faith is an essential element. Webster's dictionary defines the word faith as the complete trust or confidence; unquestioning belief, specifically in God.

The essence of our faith is placing our unwavering trust in a God that none of us have seen with our natural eyes. Despite this, many of us hear Him call to us within our spirits and feel His presence around us. As believers in a God that cannot be seen with our own eyes, it is imperative that we develop our trust in that same God that cannot be traced or quantified by any method of human measurement.

Applied Faith

Our faith as believers in God is rendered invalid unless it is applied and directed toward a specific goal. All throughout the Bible there are instances in which miracles were performed. In each of these cases the faith of the afflicted individuals was applied and directed toward a specific goal. One of my favorite passages of scripture is found in chapter 5 of the gospel of Mark. This powerful passage centers upon the story of a twelve-year-old girl having her life restored and a woman with a twelve-year issue of blood both being healed on the same day by Jesus. Both of these examples exemplify the concept of applied faith in two distinct forms.

In verse 23 of Mark chapter 5 we read that a ruler named Jairus came to Jesus and informed Him that his twelve-year-old daughter was dying. He told Jesus, "Come and lay your hands on her, that she may be healed, and she will live." Jesus and His disciples then proceeded to follow him to his home where his daughter laid.

As Jesus was making his way towards the home of Jairus, a woman with a twelve-year flow of blood came from behind Him and touched the hem of His garment. Jesus felt her touch and said, "Somebody touched Me, for I perceived power going out from Me." The woman in an example of the power of applied faith spoke the following words to herself, "if only I may touch the hem of His garment, I shall be made well." After the woman, informed Jesus that she was the person who touched Him, Jesus turned around and told her, "be of good cheer, daughter; your faith has made you well" (Mark 5:23).

As a direct result of the application of her faith, the woman was healed by Jesus immediately. What if she would have stayed at home that day knowing that Jesus was in her city? What if she would not have believed that Jesus possessed the power to heal her of her affliction? She would have most likely spent the rest of her life never being relieved of her blood flow issue. She knew precisely where to go to receive her miracle and she also knew that the application of her faith would represent the vehicle through which it would be received.

I believe that when Jesus felt the power of her faith, He knew that it reflected her belief that God could do what seemed to be impossible. Jesus recognized the spirit of her faith because faith in itself is a divine concept. This divine concept is given by God to each of His children as a means by which to summon His power. The fingerprint of faith is encoded with the DNA of God. When people witness the power of God working as a result of applied faith, it leaves behind traces of divine evidence that cannot be denied. When we witness that power at work ourselves, it often serves as a reinforcement of our own faith.

As we read further into Mark chapter 5 and reach verse 35, Jesus is interrupted as He was speaking to the woman with the blood flow issue. He is informed that the twelve-year-old daughter of Jairus had indeed died. Jesus then turned to Jairus and said, "do not be afraid only believe" (Mark 5:35). As Jesus made His way to the home of Jairus, He allowed only His disciples Peter, James and John the brother of James to follow Him.

When Jesus finally reached the home of Jairus, the man who first summoned his presence, there was a crowd of mourners that had gathered. In verse 39 of chapter 5 Jesus says to them, "do not weep she is not dead, but sleeping." Jesus then proceeded to put all of the mourners out of the house and entered in to where the girl was laying. He told the girl, "I say to you arise," and she immediately arose and walked (Mark 5: 39-42).

Two Types of Faith

There were two types of faith that were displayed within the examples found in this passage of scripture. The first is the power of faith that an individual can have in causing the power of God to move on their behalf. The second is the power of others having faith on behalf of an individual who needs a touch from God.

In the case of the woman with the blood flow issue, the application of her own faith attracted the attention of Jesus and compelled Him to heal her infirmity. In the case of Jairus's daughter, she was unable to apply her own faith to attract the restoration power of Jesus. Her father Jairus had to apply his own faith in the healing power of Jesus on behalf of his daughter. This particular example illustrates the importance of having people in our lives that can stand in the gap and believe that God will activate His power on our behalf. It exemplifies the importance of how our prayers for other people can cause the power of God to work in their lives.

In our modern time, we do not have the luxury of having Jesus Christ walking the earth in human form and performing miracles on a daily basis. His physical presence departed from this earth nearly 2,000 years ago. As He ascended into heaven, He left on earth a fragment of His divine power for each of us to use. This particular power can only be accessed through the application of our faith.

This divine presence is with us in the form of the Holy Spirit who descended into earth when the physical presence of Jesus ascended into heaven.

In the book of John chapter 16 verse 7 Jesus states, "Nevertheless I tell you the truth. It is to your advantage that I go away; for if I do not go away, the Helper will not come to you; but if I depart, I will send Him to you." In verses 12-14 he goes on to state, "I still have many things to say to you, but you cannot bear them now. However, when He, the Spirit of truth, has come, He will guide you into all truth; for He will not speak on His own authority, but whatever He hears He will speak; and He will tell you things to come. He will glorify Me, for He will take of what is Mine and declare it to you."

Just as the power of Jesus was activated as a response to faith when He inhabited the earth, the power of the Holy Spirit is activated by the application of faith in our modern times as well. The life of Jesus on earth was confined to the geographical area bordering the Mediterranean Sea that is in modern times commonly referred to as the Middle East. The Holy Spirit contains no geographical boundaries and is alive and actively working every minute of every day. There is nothing on this earth that can match the power that He possesses.

No matter who holds the position of President in the United States of America, whether they are a Democrat or a Republican, The Holy Spirit is the master mentor that will lead each of us to success. The election of Donald Trump to the office of President has many Americans feeling like Jairus did in Mark chapter 5, when he received word that his daughter had died. They are unable to fathom how his election could have happened and are cautiously pessimistic that economic and social conditions will deteriorate in this country as a result of the 2016 Presidential election. For others, the election of Donald Trump represented a political garment touch and they are optimistic that it will improve the landscape of the United States. There are stark contrasts in regards to the opinions of both groups and each of them has their reasons for feeling pessimistic or optimistic in how they feel the next several years will unfold.

God Is In Control

As of today, only God knows exactly what the next several years will hold. As people of faith our trust should be placed in God and not in any man. Donald Trump is a man in a powerful position that will represent our country all over the world. We hope that he will represent our country well and do the right things on our behalf. Only he can control his own actions. Advisors and constituents may desire for him to govern in a particular manner, but ultimately his decisions will be his own. I pray that he chooses to make wise decisions under the guidance of God's spirit. It is impossible for us as humans to legislate the moral compass of any individual, but we must know that God is always in control.

Our positions in this country may not be as prominent or as powerful as the one Donald Trump has been elected to. The decisions that he and our other elected officials make will certainly affect our lives, but they will not control them. No matter who is in office, God sent each of us to maximize the potential of our own lives.

Some of you have children who question what the presidency of Donald Trump will mean for their future. They are afraid and many of you are unsure of what to say in your effort to comfort them. Tell them that God is on their side. Let them know that their faith in Him represents the currency by which blessings are received. Make sure they understand that their faith is invalid unless it is applied and directed towards a specific goal.

The presidency of Donald Trump does not define the lives or the goals of any of us. His presence may be a perceived obstruction to progress but in life there are no circumstances that can imprison the determined will of a child of God. Donald Trump made his plan and succeeded. God has empowered you with His own spirit to do the same thing.

Until we as black Americans decide to collectively and schematically value education and ownership more than we value entertainment and consumerism, we will still be left holding on to three fifths of the American Dream. It is now our collective responsibility to get there with or without the support of any political figure. You must believe that your life has a special meaning. The world uses labels to classify who you are. God uses favor to validate your existence. Your faith in God is the ultimate display of your trust in Him.

My Life

I was a fighter from the day I was born into this world. For the first two weeks of my life I was attached to a life support machine, unable to breathe on my own. This was a complication of my premature birth. My mother was warned by Doctors that I may not develop normally and that I would have a difficult time growing up. She refused to believe in their professional opinions and instead turned to her faith. That was over thirty years ago and by the grace of God I have been breathing on my own since then and now through this book, I am breathing life into your dreams today.

If you live long enough on this earth, you will come to the realization that life is not easy. There will be times of highs and lows. There will be times when your presence will provide hope for others. There will be other times when you will need someone else to provide hope for you.

The most important thing that I learned at an early age was to have faith in God. He represents my source. The second most important thing that I learned was to believe in the abilities that He gave me. They represent my resources. Your knowledge of these two elements will keep you moving forward when the vicissitudes of life attempt to prevent you from advancing.

Each of us only gets one chance to live on this earth. The fact that you are alive and functioning is a blessing that so many people take for granted each day. God did not create you to come to this earth and spend your whole life fighting to survive the circumstances of it. You were created to live out a specific purpose and to be successful in doing so.

Your walk with God is an individual journey. The people that He places in your life are there to enrich that journey. They are there for you to consistently shine as a radiant reflection of God's love. Your life is a blessing from God and it should be used to bless the lives of the individuals that you encounter. It is my sincere hope that you learn to plant seeds of faith, and apply those seeds with your knowledge of God's power.

Chapter 9 Questions

1. Do I trust in God wholeheartedly?

2. Is my faith targeted toward a specific goal?

3. Do I have the faith to believe God for someone else's miracle?

Chapter 10

Belief, Sight and Achievement

True success happens in life when we are able to match the desires of our wants with the design of God's will. The uncovering of this process takes communicating with Him through prayer. It is through our prayers that we are able to know when God is speaking to us. To hear the voice of God our ego must be quieted in order for our spirit to clearly hear from Him. In the book of Psalms chapter 46 verse 10 it states, "Be still and know that I am God." Daily practice of prayer and meditation is an excellent way to keep us in the presence of God. They are the foundations of faith and are simple ways that allow us to apply our faith. In this chapter, I will share key steps that will assist you in aligning your wants with the will of God for your life.

If God puts a dream in your heart, He desires to see it fulfilled. He ultimately needs to see if you have enough faith to believe in His promise. This is where having a prayer life is crucial. Each of us has the power of God living on the inside of us. This power is in the form of the Holy Spirit. The Holy Spirit was given to us to connect us with the power of heaven. In order for the power of God to effectively work, you must know exactly what you believe God for.

Belief

If you ask many individuals what they believe God for, you will often get the following two responses: *I don't know what I believe God for or I am hoping that He can help me to survive day to day*. These responses attract both supernatural impotence and daily survival respectively.

You must go to God with the firm expectation that He will answer your prayers. When you go to Him you must be clear to Him about what you believe that He will manifest in your life. In order for faith to be effective, it needs an object of focus. Placing faith behind an unknown desire is the equivalent of trying to cut grass with a snow blower. Employing faith in order to live a life of survival will only promote a life of survival and not success. Doubt and fear are responsible for delaying and denying more dreams than any other culprit. They must be controlled in order for the power of God to reach its highest level of effectiveness.

Impatience often sets in when the object of our faith is not achieved within the timetable that we set for it to be accomplished. Waiting on God to move is a difficult time in which our faith is tested to measure its strength and endurance. God is responsible for sending blessings into our lives; He is also in control of when they are sent to us.

When faith is applied there is often a period of waiting until God's blessing is manifested. There are times when answered prayers are manifested within a matter of minutes or hours. Sometimes it may take months or even years from the conception of a dream until it is manifested. This is when we must keep our faith and hold on to the promise of God. In the book of Mark chapter 11 verse 24 Jesus states, "Therefore I say to you, whatever things you ask when you pray, believe that you receive them, and you will have them."

Chinese Bamboo Tree

On the continent of Asia there is a tree commonly known as the Chinese Bamboo Tree. This tree when it is fully developed can reach a height of almost 100 feet. What makes the Chinese Bamboo Tree unique is not its height or the geographical location where it grows. What makes the tree unique is the fact that it does not sprout from the ground during its first four years alive. During the fifth year, the tree grows to its full height within a matter of weeks.

Our faith operates in the same manner as the Chinese Bamboo Tree. The tree develops underground in a dark place devoid of sunlight. The law of nature dictates that as long as it is properly nourished and left undisturbed during the five-year growth process, the Chinese Bamboo Tree will develop as it is created to do. Our faith is not something that can be seen visually. It is a belief that cannot be quantified by any unit of scientific measurement. Faith in itself is invisible but its results are immeasurable.

God uses our faith as the seed to develop our blessings beyond the plane of our vision. We nourish our faith through prayer and the belief that God will eventually manifest the desire of our heart. During the process of our blessing being developed, it is imperative that we do not allow fear and doubt to disturb our belief in what God is manifesting on our behalf. We must remember that faith is a process and not a singular moment. The Chinese Bamboo Tree first begins its life as a seed before it is manifested into a tree. Our blessings begin as seeds of faith before they are manifested into the reality of our lives.

The Faith of Caleb

In the book of Numbers chapter 13, we read about Caleb, one of the twelve spies sent by Moses to spy out the land of Canaan. Caleb brought a faith filled report to Moses and believed that the Israelites were able to possess the Promised Land. Due to the negative report of ten of his fellow spies, he spent the next forty years wandering in the wilderness with the Israelites as a punishment from God for their lack of faith in His promise to them.

Forty years later, Caleb along with Joshua, and a new generation of Israelites, finally enter the Promised Land. During the period of waiting, Caleb never lost his faith in God. In the book of Joshua chapter 14 verse 7 he states, "I was forty years old when Moses the servant of the Lord sent me from Kadesh Barnea to spy out the land, and I brought back word to him as it was in my heart. Nevertheless, my brethren who went up with me made the heart of the people melt, but I wholly followed the Lord my God."

In verses 11-14 of Joshua chapter 14 he goes on to state, "As yet I am strong this day as on the day that Moses sent me; just as my strength was then, so now is my strength for war, both for going out and for coming in. Now therefore, give me this mountain of which the Lord spoke in that day; for you heard in that day how the Anakim were there, and that the cities were great and fortified. It may be that the Lord will be with me, and I shall be able to drive them out as the Lord said." And Joshua blessed him, and gave Hebron to Caleb the son of Jephunneh as an inheritance. Hebron therefore became the inheritance of Caleb the son of Jephunneh the Kenizzite to this day, because he wholly followed the Lord God of Israel (Joshua 14:11-14).

Sight

Caleb held on to the belief that he would enter into the Promised Land and possess the mountain of Hebron. Before he could possess the mountain, he had to first see himself possessing it. His eventual possession of the mountain was first formed as a belief. His belief was then transformed into a mental picture while he waited for God to manifest his blessing. Caleb's example shows us that our belief must become something that we can visually see before it is manifested unto us.

In our modern times, the method that Caleb used is still reliable. In our modern times, we have the added benefit of using photographs and pictures as a means to clearly visualize the objects of our faith. Some people even like to create vision boards or write out goal lists which feature the desires that they believe that God has placed in their hearts. I believe that this is an excellent method that will allow you to keep your goals at the forefront of your mind while God is orchestrating the methods of their manifestation. It is a way to also apply your faith and stay determined and disciplined while waiting on God to move on your behalf.

The Bible speaks about the importance of writing our vision down. "Write the vision and make it plain on tablets, that he may run who reads it. For the vision is yet for an appointed time; But at the end it will speak, and it will not lie. Though it tarries, wait for it; because it will surely come, it will not tarry" (Habakkuk 2:2-3). I am a firm believer that there is power in visualization. Writing out your vision takes time and effort but I can assure you that it is worth it.

Achievement

There is truly no good thing that God cannot bring about in your life. The blessings of God are granted in the direct result of your faith. "Therefore, it is of faith that it might be according to grace, so that the promise might be sure to all the seed, not only to those who are of the law, but also to those who are of the faith of Abraham, who is the father of us all in the presence of Him whom he believed God, who gives life to the dead and calls those things which do not exist as though they did" (Romans 4:16-17).

When the object of our faith is achieved it is imperative that we thank God for it. Whether you know it or not there is someone who is watching your life closely. They are looking to see if your belief in God is real and if He truly is a God that blesses His children. God ultimately blesses us in order to strengthen our faith in Him and to strengthen the faith of those who witness what He chooses to perform in our lives.

Caleb was rewarded by God as a result of his faithfulness to His promise. Caleb chose to believe in the promise of faith despite having to wait many years to see its fulfillment. What will future generations say about the testament of your faithfulness to the promises of God? The names of Shaphat and Igal are unknown today. They were two of the twelve spies who chose to relay a negative report about the Promised Land to Moses despite God's promise to deliver it to them. They saw the same things that Caleb and Joshua saw, but they did not share their level of faith in the true and living God.

Shaphat and Igal allowed the spirit of fear to prevent them from believing in God's promise. They were among the children of Israel that perished in the wilderness before being able to make it into the Promised Land. Applied faith can make you a history maker as in the case of Joshua and

Caleb, while applied fear can make you a history lesson as in the case of Shaphat and Igal. I encourage you to keep your faith strong and God will ultimately position your life on the right side of history. Believe that the object of your faith is possible to attain, visualize it as being possible and God will assist your efforts in achieving it.

Chapter 10 Questions

1. Do I pray every day?
   _____
   _____
   _____
   _____

2. Do I possess a patient level of faith?
   _____
   _____
   _____
   _____

3. Do I believe that my wants match God's will?
   _____
   _____
   _____
   _____

Chapter 11

From Belief to Blessing

Things that are truly worth having in life must be earned. Anything that is eligible to be earned must first be believed for. During your lifetime, there will be times that you will know beyond a shadow of a doubt that God has blessed you according to your faith. It is impossible to receive the blessings of God without having the faith to believe that they are possible. Even with the evidence of God blessing you in the past, there will still be times that doubt may creep into your mind and cause you to wonder if God will bless you in the future.

There may be a promise that you believe that God will bring to pass that has not manifested itself yet. You have prayed for it and believed in faith and nothing seems to be happening. In your heart, you know that God placed this particular desire within you that will not go away. This desire may also seem to be impossible to accomplish.

For some of you the promise could entail starting a new business, for others it could be paying off a significant amount of debt or being healed of an affliction. Your prayer could be for God to bless you with a spouse or to repair a relationship. It could even be for God to bless you with a child or for Him to perform a miracle in the life of someone you love. I don't know what it is that you are standing in faith for and believing God to bless you with. When you are faced with this situation there are several things that it is imperative that you keep at the forefront of your mind.

The first thing is, God loves you and He hears your prayers. The second thing is, a blessing delayed is not a blessing denied. In times like these, God is often showing you the importance of trusting in His timing for your life. God may be using the time of delay to test your level of faith in Him and using it as a means to compel you to mature spiritually. He may also be working on putting the right people in the proper position to bring your blessing to fruition.

The third thing that you must keep at the forefront of your mind is your faith. Thoughts truly do become things. Faith is the universal key that unlocks the blessings stored in heaven that are attached to your name. "But without faith it is impossible to please Him, for he who comes to God must believe that He is, and that He is a rewarder of those who diligently seek Him" (Hebrews 11:6).

The Persistent Faith of Jacob

In Genesis chapter 32 it details the account of Jacob, the grandson of Abraham, wrestling with a Man who is presumed by many biblical scholars as a pre-incarnate appearance of Jesus Christ. Jacob wrestled with the Man all night long. Despite being overmatched in his struggle with the Man, he did not give up. The wrestling match was so rough that Jacob's hip socket was dislodged. Despite the pain he felt, Jacob refused to let go of the Man. In verse 26 of chapter 32, Jacob states, "I will not let You go unless You bless me." So He said to him, "What is your name?" "He said, Jacob." And He said, "Your name shall no longer be called Jacob, but Israel; for you have struggled with God and with men, and have prevailed."

This illustration in the life of Jacob is an example to us that the rewards of faith are often the result of fierce determination and inspired persistence. Even though Jacob faced pain in his battle with the Man, he held on to his faith that God would bless him as long as he stayed focused and did not give up on the promise within his heart. Jacob could have quit at any point during the wrestling match or allowed himself to be distracted by elements outside of the match. He was able to stay focused because he knew that the reward of God's blessing would be found on the other side of his place of struggle. To cross the river of struggle from the point of faith to the place of blessing, Jacob used a raft of sacrifice to transition his moment of faith into a movement of God's blessings.

No matter what dream or goal you are wrestling with today, it is imperative that you understand that the God of Jacob is working on your behalf today. He will respond to the call of your faith. He is still blessing His children and desires to see you have a successful life. Are you willing to hold on to Him until He blesses you? Are you willing to stay focused and persistent in the pursuit of what you believe that He is going to do? Is there something that you must sacrifice that will carry you from the initial point of faith to your destined place of blessing?

Your life carries with it a tremendous amount of value. God loves you and desires to see you prosperous and blessed. The blessings of God are the advertisements of the benefits of faith. God does not necessarily need anyone to rent billboards on the sides of highways in order to advertise the benefits of serving Him. He just needs His children to simply explain to others about how He has blessed their lives according to their faith in Him.

There is a little bit of Jacob in each of us, but our faith must be tried and tested for us to become Israel. Our God may not change your name, but He will change your situation if you are determined to be blessed no matter with whom or what you may be forced to wrestle with. Just hold on to your faith and believe beyond a shadow of a doubt that God is safely moving you closer to your place of blessing.

When Jacob was holding on to the angel, he was standing on a previous promise that God had made to him. In verse 12 of Genesis chapter 28, Jacob dreamed of a ladder that reached from heaven to earth and had angels ascending and descending on it. "And behold, the Lord stood above it and said: I am the Lord God of Abraham your father and the God of Isaac; the land on which you lie I will give to you and your descendants." In verse 15 of Genesis chapter 28, God states to Jacob, "Behold, I am with you and will keep you wherever you go, and will bring you back to this land; for I will not leave you until I have done what I have spoken to you."

Just as He was with Jacob, God is always faithful when it comes to granting His promises. The reason that Jacob was confident when he encountered the angel in Genesis chapter 32 was due to his belief in the promise that God originally gave to him in chapter 28. The manner in which Jacob refused to let go of the angel until He blessed him is the same manner in which we must hold on to our faith while we await God's blessings in our lives.

When God gave Jacob the promise to give him the land on which he was standing in Genesis chapter 28 verse 13; He did not reveal to Jacob the method of how He was going to bring the promise to pass. Jacob took God at His word because he had seen the clear evidence of God's work in his own life and was aware of what God had done for his father Isaac and his grandfather Abraham.

Think for a moment about how God has blessed you in your life. There are situations that you can look back upon and clearly know that the hand of God moved on your behalf. If God has been good to you in the past, these tangible advertisements of the benefits of faith should serve as reminders of his undying love for you.

You must believe that your future will be greater than your past. If God blessed the lives of Abraham, Isaac and Jacob and kept His word to them, it is incumbent upon you to have faith that He will do the same thing for you. Jesus Christ is the same yesterday, today, and forever (Hebrews 13:8). The blessings of God are timeless and do not carry dates of expiration for individuals who apply the currency of faith as a secured deposit of their unwavering trust in Him.

Showing Gratitude

One day several years ago I woke up feeling both disappointed with both God and myself. My feeling of disappointment was due to my belief that my life had not turned out how I would have hoped it would have up until that point. I was living a life in which I was frustrated by the gap between my expectations of where I felt I should be in life, versus the place where my life currently was.

This was due to the fact that I was looking at how God was blessing the individuals around me and I was feeling that God had forgotten about the dreams within my heart. I didn't lose my faith in God, but it was a time in my life that challenged my patience with His timing. At that time in my life I had to learn to show gratitude for my own life and realize that I was already immensely blessed.

For some people, the job that I had could have represented the dream opportunity that they needed to pay their bills. My presence on that job was also an opportunity for God to reflect His light through me to the people that I encountered there daily. The fact that I was able to walk and even run when I felt like it is something that many people pray to God for daily. I had a car to drive every day which was the dream of someone else who had to walk everywhere they went because they were unable to afford their own transportation.

I reminded myself that there were people sleeping on the streets and in shelters praying to God to someday live in a place of their own. The small apartment that I lived in protected me from the elements. I had eyes to see the world around me and ears that could hear the sounds within it. These are gifts that others wish they could possess.

I also had the freedom to come and go as I pleased without being confined to a specific corner of the earth. I thought about the innocent people imprisoned who would give anything to experience the freedoms that I had daily. I had people in my life that I was blessed to be able to give love to and receive love back from. It made me remember that there were people in the world who felt alone without someone showing them that they cared for them. Most of all, I was grateful for my relationship with God and the knowledge that He loved me. The acknowledgement of my current blessings taught me to be grateful for what I presently had while I waited for God to work out the future circumstances of my life.

I learned that the key to experience greater blessings from God was found within my ability to be grateful for the blessings that He had already provided for me. In life, we must learn to never take the people and things that God has blessed us with for granted. Even though we know that God has done great things for us in the past and we expect for Him to do great things for us in the future, we must be grateful for what He is currently doing for us right now.

Your life right now may not be where you envisioned that it would be years ago. You may be facing struggles and disappointments right now. You may feel that your future is uncertain. Know that you are blessed today. In the book of Lamentations, the prophet Jeremiah wrote emphatically at length about the faithfulness of God. In chapter three he wrote, "Through the Lord's mercies we are not consumed, because His compassions fail not. They are new every morning; Great is Your faithfulness" (Lamentations 3:22-23).

The same God that Jeremiah wrote about is working out the details of your dreams today. I encourage you to stay faithful in your belief in what He will perform in your future. I also implore you to be thankful for what He has done in your past. Most of all, I ask that you please be grateful for what He is currently doing for you today.

Chapter 11 Questions

1. Do I believe that God hears my prayers?
   _____
   _____
   _____
   _____
   _____

2. Is my faith persistent?
   _____
   _____
   _____
   _____
   _____

3. What am I willing to sacrifice as a sign of my faith?
   _____
   _____
   _____
   _____
   _____

Chapter 12

Remember Your Why

In the first chapter of this book, I shed some light upon the negative aspects of what I was exposed to while growing up in Detroit, Michigan. During that same time period, there were positive aspects that I was exposed to while growing up that greatly influenced my personal growth and development. As a child, my reading and comprehension scores were consistently ranked in the top percentile for my age group. It was evident to my mother and teachers that I possessed gifts that allowed me to excel in the area of language arts. I developed an affinity for reading thought provoking material and for hearing the words of powerful orators.

During my formative years, motivational speaker Les Brown was living and working in the city of Detroit. I began to study his speeches and the methods that he employed to impact audiences through the power of his words. Around the same time period that I began to study the speeches of Les Brown, my mother began attending Hartford Memorial Baptist Church which at the time was pastored by Dr. Charles G. Adams. Every Sunday morning, I would sit mesmerized by the didactic dispensations of scripture that Dr. Adams would exegete.

Dr. Adams became my homiletical hero and Les Brown became my oratorical role model. As a result of my exposure to their influence, I began to believe that one day my name would be mentioned amongst theirs for my ability to speak words that empowered and uplifted others. I also began to visualize myself someday standing in front of large crowds and being able to share my oratorical gift with them.

Over time, as I developed my affinity for reading thought provoking material, there were two writers whose work I took a keen interest in. The first writer was Mitch Albom, the longtime Detroit Free Press columnist and best-selling author. I began to study the subject matter of his columns and the style in which he wrote them. During that same time period, I also began to read books written by my fellow Detroit native, Dr. Michael Eric Dyson. I found his writing style and subject matter to be in the same vein as the oratorical preaching style of Dr. Adams.

Dr. Dyson and Mitch Albom became my linguistic role models, and I began to develop my own writing style by incorporating elements from their styles. I began to believe that someday my name would be mentioned amongst those of Mitch Albom and Dr. Dyson for my ability to write words that empowered and uplifted others. I began to see myself as a future best-selling author whose writing would someday improve the conditions in this world.

The words of my oratorical and linguistic role models inspired me to expand my imagination and challenged me to elevate my thinking above the reality of my life in the ghetto. Inspired by the power of their words, I began to dream of a life beyond the corner of Mack Avenue and Fairview Street. I formed a belief in my mind that a world class writer and motivational speaker would emerge from my neighborhood and I believed in my heart that it would be me. I never knew how long it would take for me to achieve my dreams. All I had back then was my faith in God and the vision of my future that He gave me. No matter what trials I faced or how many years passed, I never let go of that vision. I always remembered my why. I discovered over time that the road to greatness is paved with the stones of consistent excellence.

In my life, I have learned that there will be seasons in life in which the days, weeks and months will just seem to run together. These are times of uncertainty in which you will feel that you are stuck between the promises of your dream and the reality of its achievement. In these seasons, you must remember your why. God created your life to have a unique purpose and the dreams that He gives you must have a unique purpose as well. There is someone who will benefit from the fulfillment of that which God has placed inside of you.

For example, if your dream is to write a book, think about the people that will be inspired by your work. Your life experiences or the special way that you can explain a concept may be exactly what someone else may need to reach the next level in life that God is challenging them to grow to. In the book of Proverbs chapter 18 verse 16 it states, "A man's gift makes room for him and brings him before great men." Your specific gift when applied with faith is the passageway to your dreams being fulfilled.

The Dream

The biblical narrative of the life of Joseph is an example of how a person's gift and the application of their faith can move the hand of God to work on their behalf. There was a period of twenty-two years between Joseph's dream and its manifestation. For twenty-two years Joseph stood in faith and never gave up on the promise of God. He stayed faithful to God and God stayed faithful to him.

Genesis chapter 5 records the dream of Joseph, it states, Now Joseph had a dream, and he told it to his brothers; and they hated him even more. So he said to them, "Please hear this dream which I dreamed: There we were, binding sheaves in the field. Then behold, my sheaf rose and also stood upright; and indeed your sheaves stood all around and bowed down to my sheaf." And his brothers said to him, "Shall you indeed reign over us? Or shall you indeed have dominion over us?" So they hated him even more for his dreams and his words (Genesis 5:5-8).

Joseph's brothers plotted to kill him after he told them about his dream of him ruling over them. Joseph's life was spared by his brother Reuben who first convinced his brothers to leave him in a pit. He was then sold into slavery at the behest of his brother Judah who sought to profit from abandoning Joseph. Joseph eventually was sent to Egypt where he spent the next thirteen years in captivity (See Genesis 37:21-36).

During his time in captivity, Joseph never forgot his dream no matter how difficult the circumstances may have been for him. Even though he did not know the timing of God, he believed in the accuracy of His promise to him. The dream of Joseph eventually being in a position of leadership over his brothers was his why. I believe it was his why that kept him moving forward during his years in captivity. Joseph continued to show honor to God by developing and applying his gift during his years in captivity.

Even though he was a victim of circumstance, he made the conscious decision to live as a champion of faith. Are your current circumstances imprisoning your dreams?

You may feel that the dreams that God has placed inside of you are beyond your reach. You may feel as if God is not moving expeditiously enough on your behalf. For Joseph, it took twenty-two long years from the birth of his dream, until it was fulfilled. During the time between his captivity and freedom, it was applied faith that carried Joseph through it all. Each time that he used his gift, it was an application of his faith. The application of his faith eventually led to God seeing fit to promote him from beneath the outhouse of oppression and into the penthouse of promise.

The Gift of Joseph

In the book of Genesis, the example of Joseph's life provides us with clear cut evidence of how a person's gift can make room for them and bring them before great men. I often wonder how Joseph may have felt each day waking up for thirteen years in captivity. Each day he did work that was less than his intellectual capacity and light years away from the promise that God placed inside of him.

Day after day, week after week, month after month and year after year, he toiled in obscurity. I am sure there were days in which he wanted to hide and not have to face the reality of his circumstances. There may have been weeks that he may have questioned if God was too busy to help him. There may have been months in which he wondered if he had heard God correctly. There may have even been years in which he wondered if God had forgotten about him altogether.

The book of Genesis does not record the innermost thoughts of Joseph. They will forever be a mystery known only between him and God. Even though we do not know the thoughts of Joseph, the book of Genesis fortunately provides us with the narrative of his actions. His actions show a man who never stopped believing in God despite being trapped living in a reality of unfair occurrences and unfulfilled promise.

The life of Joseph proves to us that even though the promises of God may be delayed in our timing, they are right on schedule according to Him. Through each day of his time in captivity, God's hand covered the life of Joseph and He prospered him in a place of desolate dreams. Joseph was used by God to reflect His light in a dark place. "The keeper of the prison did not look into anything that was under Joseph's authority, because the Lord was with him; and whatever he did, the Lord made it prosper" (Genesis 39:23).

Just as Joseph used his gift to reflect God's light in a dark place, you possess the same ability as well. You may currently be in a predicament that may cause you to wonder why you are currently where you are. It could be on a job, it could be within your family dynamic or it could even be behind prison walls just as Joseph was. You may be the only representative of God where you are currently placed. You have the choice to use your gift to bloom or make the decision to use your circumstances as an excuse to be buried right where you are. Joseph used his gift as a mechanism that enabled him to bloom while in captivity.

Joseph's greatest gift was his ability to understand dreams and interpret them. Ironically, that same gift is what caused him to be sold into slavery by his brothers, and that same gift led to his promotion out of the prison and into the palace of the Pharaoh. The plight of Joseph is empirical evidence that the hand of God can elevate the lives of any of His children no matter where they are.

There were three things that led Joseph out of the prison and into the palace. The three things were: God's favor, Joseph's gift to interpret dreams and his belief in the manifestation of the original dream that God placed within him when he was seventeen years of age. Joseph's why was reaching the fulfillment of the dream that would show his brothers bowing down to him. Joseph was successful long before he rose to prominence as the second in command in Egypt. His success stemmed from his keen ability to use his gift in a place that only a handful of people would see it in action.

Joseph did not have a prestigious title, nor was he a member of an influential family in the land of Egypt. He was just a young Hebrew man equipped with a gift to interpret dreams and empowered by a God whose grace covered him. He was faithful to God and worked diligently in the prison to reflect God's spirit in each task that he undertook. Through the power of faith, Joseph learned how to successfully balance his Hebrew identity with his Egyptian citizenship.

We serve a God who rewards individuals that live their lives determined to make the most of what they have to work with. Jesus alluded to this when he told the parable of the talents in Matthew chapter 25. He stated, "Well done, good and faithful servant; you were faithful over a few things, I will make you ruler over many things. Enter into the joy of your lord" (Matthew 25:21). You must believe that God will reward your efforts even if you feel that the individuals around you do not recognize it. God has the power to use anyone in your path as the catalyst for your elevation.

In the life of Joseph, God used a butler from the palace of the Pharaoh to assist Joseph. When the Pharaoh experienced a dream that caused him concern, there was no one in the land of Egypt that could be found to interpret his dream. It was then that his butler remembered a prisoner named Joseph who successfully interpreted a dream for him two years prior (Genesis 41:12). This was the moment that Joseph's life changed for the better.

All the years of toiling in obscurity were put to an end when the Pharaoh's butler finally remembered Joseph and his unique gift of interpreting dreams. When Joseph was summoned by Pharaoh, he humbly gave God the credit for his gift. In Genesis chapter 41 verse 16 he states, "It is not in me; God will give Pharaoh an answer of peace." Pharaoh sensed the spirit of God within Joseph and elevated him within one day from a common prisoner to the second in command ruling in the land of Egypt (Genesis 41:40).

There may be someone reading this who may feel imprisoned by their current circumstances. The dream that God placed inside of you seems to be impossible to reach. You could spend your days feeling as if you are toiling in obscurity. You could be facing a health challenge, a financial difficulty or be incarcerated behind the mental walls of fear. I urge you to know that your life does have a unique purpose and that your why can be achieved.

We live in a world in which everything seems to have a price attached to it. Your why is no different than any other commodity in that respect. Its price is not paid with gold or any form of paper currency. It is paid through your unwavering faith in the power of God and your unrelenting belief in the application of the unique gift that He blessed you with to empower and uplift the world with.

I do believe that as in the life of Joseph, there are seasons when we will face unfair circumstances and tests that seem to challenge the validity of our faith. These are the times that God shows His reliability to us. You must internalize the fact that your gift will make room for you.

Your gift is meant to benefit the world and display the reflection of God's power simultaneously. The world needs what you specifically have to offer. You may currently be living in an environment in which your gift seems to go unnoticed. Just know that God sees you and that He will place the right people in your path that need to experience the application of your gift.

Joseph may have been physically imprisoned but God supplied the wings of prosperity that his gift needed to elevate him above his lowly circumstances. God used the recommendation of the Pharaoh's butler which directly led to Joseph's unprecedented promotion to being the second in command in Egypt. Who will you encounter today that needs to experience the full benefit of your gift? Joseph remembered his why and he kept his faith. In turn, God kept His promise to him and stayed faithful to His word to him. If you remember your why, the God of Joseph will keep His promise to you as well. I implore you to keep your faith in Him and He will keep His word to you.

Chapter 12 Questions

1. What does my why represent to me?
   _____
   _____
   _____
   _____

2. Do I believe that my gift will make room for me?
   _____
   _____
   _____
   _____

3. Am I using my gift while I wait for God to promote me?
   _____
   _____
   _____
   _____

Chapter 13

The Power of The Anointing

All through the scriptures the mark of God's favor is represented by His anointing. The I AM power of God is covered with His anointing. The oil generated from crushed olives is the physical representation of the anointing. Olive oil was used in ancient times to represent the flow of God's blessings. It is also used today in the Christian faith in the same manner. Without the olive being crushed, it is impossible for the oil to flow out of it.

Our lives as children of God are similar to that of the olive. In order for the anointing of God to flow freely through us, the desires of our flesh must be crushed. When this happens, you will become fervent in your desire to do the will of God for your life. In the book of Romans chapter 14 verse 13 the Apostle Paul wrote, "But put on the Lord Jesus Christ, and make no provision for the flesh, to fulfill its lusts."

None of us who lives on this earth is perfect. As human beings created in the image of God, we all make mistakes and we all have shortcomings and imperfections. The power of God's anointing is what keeps us striving to reflect the perfection of His spirit while reconciling the imperfection of our own flesh. This is a daily process that we as believers in God should continuously seek to become successful at managing.

Balancing Spirit and Flesh

A large ego restricts the flow of the anointing. A large ego is the result of uncontrolled pride. Increasing our level of humility will decrease the size of our ego. This is a process that God undertakes within us by force, either through unforeseen circumstances of life that involuntarily humble us, or through the invitation of our prayers to Him. The decrease of the ego creates the necessary space for God's spirit to flow without restriction within us.

The ego is powered by the desires of the flesh. The spirit of God within us is powered by the flow of the anointing. The ego creates circumstances that the anointing has the ability to remedy. In the book of Isaiah chapter 10 verse 27 it states, "It shall come to pass in that day that his burden will be taken away from your shoulder, and his yoke from your neck, and the yoke will be destroyed because of the anointing oil."

In our lives, there are elements that will attempt to cause us to drift away from the will of God for our lives. They are often found in unhealthy addictions that cause us to lose our focus. These addictions create strongholds that cause us to flagrantly indulge in the desires of what the world deems to be popular. We begin to gain a greater sense of comfort in following the opinions of others rather than desiring to be led by the spirit of God. When this happens, it is easy to become drawn into a lifestyle that features the false benefits of secularity.

You must remember that your life is not your own. God created you to fulfill a specific purpose on this earth. You were created to fulfill this purpose, despite your flaws, which are a function of your humanity. Each of us belongs to Him. In his first letter to the Corinthians the Apostle Paul wrote, "Or do you not know that your body is the temple of the Holy Spirit who is in you, whom you have from God, and you are not your own? For you were bought at a price; therefore glorify God in your body and in your spirit, which are God's" (1st Corinthians 6:19-20).

The anointing is presented to believers to assist us in successfully activating the I AM power that God placed inside of each of us to bring honor to Him. The anointing of God is your ticket to freedom from whatever situation that may place you in bondage. In your life today, there may be something that is holding you back from living the life that you know God desires from you. Call upon the power of Holy Spirit to fill your life with the anointing. Each of us will only get one chance on this earth to live. No one makes it out of life alive. Your life will either be a lesson for others to avoid or a blueprint for them to emulate.

Faith and The Anointing

When I was a child my mother would often use the phrase "when you are down to nothing, God is up to something." At that time in my life I couldn't fully grasp the concept that she was speaking in reference to. As I grew into adulthood, I realized that she was speaking to me in reference to faith. I had to learn that there are times that life will crush you and you will have no one to call upon but God.

There was a time in my life when I was crushed. Within a period of one day, I lost almost everything that I valued. I was faced with the decision to submit to the wants of my ego or submit to the will of God's spirit. I made the choice to silence my ego and listen to the spirit. I had to learn to humble myself, become still, and trust in God wholeheartedly.

At that time in my life I had published my first book and had traveled around the country promoting it. My situation forced me to believe in the concept of applied faith and in the power of the anointing. There were so many nights when I would wake up in the middle of the night wishing that I could talk to someone, but I was faced with the reality of having no one to call.

When those moments came I would talk to God as if He was sitting right next to me in the room. I would ask Him questions such as: What is Your plan for my life now? Why did You allow me to waste so many years and so much valuable time pouring myself into a situation that You knew would fail? What must I do to have this dark cloud lifted from my life? These questions are amongst many that I would ask God daily during that season of my life.

Up until that point in my life, I had prided myself upon being the person that so many people looked to for answers to life's questions. When life came crashing down upon me, I had no profound explanations to equip me with concrete answers to solve my own predicament. I was left humbled and looking to the sky for answers. All I had in my possession was a faith that was left shaken and bruised by my current affliction. As I look back upon that time, God had me right where He wanted me to be. He needed things to fall apart around me in order for my life to be rebuilt in the precise way that He wanted it to look. Things had to fall apart to enable Him to put them back together in the proper place.

During that time in my life, my faith in God was put to a test that I had no desire to partake in, but I ultimately had no choice but to participate in. There were so many people who had heard about what happened to me and they were now watching my life to see if I would live up to the concepts that I had written and spoken about. This was a time in my life when the words of my mother echoed so loudly within my spirit. The phrase "when you are down to nothing God is up to something," took on new life inside of me.

Each night before I went to bed, I adopted a regiment that consisted of reading my Bible, prayer and meditation. I knew that getting drunk, high or other unhealthy behaviors would only provide a temporary cover for my pain and fail to promote the divine healing that my heart needed. Each day after applying my new regiment, I began to feel stronger. I also began hear God's Holy Spirit imparting His wisdom into me. My level of faith began to increase and I began to trust in God's will more than I depended on my own plans. The anointing began to flow into my heart in a way that I had never experienced before.

As a result of this experience, I discovered the power of faith in action. God showed me that He does indeed answer the prayers of those who believe in Him. In my search for ways to heal my heart, God used the experience as a way to increase my faith in Him. I was able to learn from firsthand experience about the power of God's anointing. I realized that the spiritual corner where God's will and my prayers met represented the intersection of my blessings.

In the book of Matthew, Jesus uses the example of a fig tree to explain the concept of answered prayer. In Matthew chapter 21 verse 19, Jesus is hungry and comes upon a fig tree that is bearing leaves instead of fruit. He cursed the fig tree to never grow fruit again. Immediately after He cursed it, the fig tree withered away.

His disciples were astonished and wondered how the fig tree withered away so soon. Jesus stated to them,

"Assuredly I say to you, if you have faith and do not doubt, you will not only do what was done to the fig tree, but also if you say to this mountain, 'Be removed and be cast into the sea,' it will be done (Matthew 21:21). I encourage you to believe in the power of God's anointing. It is very real and it is very powerful. His blessings will flow to you and they will cover your life if you just trust in Him and do not doubt His power.

Elijah and The Widow

The book of 1st Kings recounts the story of the prophet Elijah and a widow from the town of Zarephath. When the Brook Cherith dried up, God sent the prophet Elijah to Zarephath and told him that He would provide for him there. Zarephath represented his new place of provision from God. As he finally reached Zarephath, he met a widow there who he asked for a cup of water and a morsel of bread (1st Kings 17: 9-11).

The widow responded to him by saying, "As the Lord your God lives, I do not have bread, only a handful of flour in a bin, and a little oil in a jar; and see, I am gathering a couple of sticks that I may go in and prepare it for myself and my son, that we may eat it, and die." Elijah then said to her, "Do not fear; go and do as you have said, but make me a small cake from it first, and bring it to me; and afterward make some for yourself and your son. For thus says the Lord God of Israel; The bin of flour shall not be used up, nor shall the jar of oil run dry until the day the Lord sends rain on the earth" (1st Kings 17: 12-16). The widow then proceeded to follow Elijah's instructions and she never ran out of flour or oil during her lifetime.

This passage of scripture teaches us about the power of trusting in God and how our trust has the power to release the overflow of anointing that will attract miracles from the hand of God. Sowing a seed into the life of someone else is what keeps the anointing flowing within your own life. Sometimes your seed may represent money, it could be time spent volunteering or just a sending a kind message to someone that God has placed in your heart to contact. Acts of unselfish love towards others will ensure that the oil flow of God's anointing will never run dry in your lifetime.

Each day that the flour bin was filled and the oil flowed uninterrupted, after she met Elijah, was a constant reminder to the widow of the benefits that trusting in God provides to those who believe in Him. It took faith and obedience in God for Elijah to leave the Brook Cherith and go to Zarephath. He went to Zarephath without hesitation because he had faith that God would provide for him there. It also took faith and obedience in God for the widow to use a portion of the last amount of her flour and oil to make a cake for Elijah first before she fed herself and her son. Her small investment of faith produced a return to her life that was incalculable.

Whenever there is a lack of something in your life that you desire, seek to find ways to plant seeds in the lives of those around you. For example, if you feel that you are lacking love in your life, make an effort to sow seeds of love into the people that you encounter. One of those individuals could possibly be the Elijah that God has sent to bless your life. The harvest that you believe God for may not come to you exactly at the time that you desire it. If you stay in faith and keep sowing seeds into the lives of others, as in the case of the widow of Zarephath, your miracle will come at the exact time that you will need it.

Chapter 13 Questions

1. Do I possess a humble spirit?
   _____
   _____
   _____
   _____

2. Am I willing to decrease the influence of my ego and increase the influence of God's spirit?
   _____
   _____
   _____
   _____

3. Is my life a lesson for others to avoid or a blueprint for them to emulate?
   _____
   _____
   _____
   _____

Chapter 14

The Great I AM

In my estimation, the most powerful phrase in literature is I AM. It is a declarative statement that contains within it an immeasurable sense of power. In the book of Exodus, we read about the life of the Hebrew leader Moses. Moses was an Israelite by birth but was adopted and raised as an Egyptian in the palace of the Pharaoh. God believed that His people had been oppressed long enough and He called upon Moses to lead them out of Egyptian oppression and into freedom in the Promised Land of Canaan.

When God called upon Moses to demand the freedom of the enslaved Israelites, he was unsure of himself. He was questioning as to why God would call upon him of all people to lead the fight to free the Israelites from their oppression. God responded to him by saying, "I will certainly be with you. And this shall be a sign to you that I have sent you: When you have brought the people out of Egypt, you shall serve God on this mountain" (Exodus 3:12).

Even after God spoke words of comfort to him, Moses was still unsure of his ability to lead the Israelites. He informed God that he was unsure what to tell the Israelites when they would eventually question him about who sent him to lead the fight for their freedom. In Exodus chapter 2 verse 14 God responds to him by saying, "I AM WHO IAM. Thus, you shall say to the children of Israel, I AM has sent me to you. Thus, you shall say to the children of Israel: The Lord God of your fathers, the God of Abraham, the God of Isaac, and the God of Jacob, has sent me to you."

In this passage of scripture, God informed Moses that He would be with him and guide him to success. Through his faith in God, Moses was able to strike the successful bicultural balance between his Hebrew identity and Egyptian citizenship. His ability to successfully strike the bicultural balance was very similar to the undertaking of his ancestor Joseph. Both of these champions of faith were well versed in the customs of Egypt which contributed greatly to their success in doing the will of God for their lives.

Generations before Moses, God entrusted Joseph to lead the Israelites into Egypt to escape famine in their Promised Land. God later entrusted Moses to secure the freedom of the Israelites away from Egypt and lead them back towards that same land in their escape from nearly 400 years of Egyptian oppression. The examples of their lives are templates of faith that black Americans can examine in our efforts to strike the successful bicultural balance between our African identity and American citizenship. This balance will successfully be accomplished through our faith in the power of I AM.

Even Jesus Christ spoke about the power of I AM. In chapter 8 of the gospel of John, Jesus encounters a group of Jewish leaders who are questioning who He really is. In one of the most powerful passages of scripture recorded in the Bible, Jesus affirms His divinity to them. In verse 53 they say to Him, "Are You greater than our father Abraham, who is dead? Who do You make Yourself out to be?" Jesus answered, "If I honor Myself, My honor is nothing. It is My Father who honors Me, of whom you say that He is your God. Yet you have not known Him, but I know Him, and if I say, I do not know Him, I shall be a liar like you; but I do know Him and keep His word.

Your father Abraham rejoiced to see My day, and he saw it and was glad." Then the Jews said to Him, "You are not yet fifty years old, and have You seen Abraham?" In response to their questions Jesus said to them, "Most assuredly, I say to you, before Abraham was, I AM" (John 8:53-58).

The God of Moses is still with you today. The I AM power that Jesus spoke about to the Jewish leaders is still alive today. In your own life, you may have been given a specific assignment like Moses was or there may be a dream inside of you that God is calling upon you to carry out. You may feel unqualified to undertake it. You may wonder where the resources will come from to help bring about your success. There may be others around you who may look at you and question if God really chose you to do something special on this earth.

In times like these it is of utter importance that you internalize the fact that, you belong to I AM and that I AM is inside of you. The Great I AM does not care how much money is in your bank account. He does not care about the color of your skin. He does not care about your height, weight or age. How popular you are on this earth does nothing to please Him either. He wants to know if you are willing to trust in Him with all your heart and be obedient to the divine commands of His will for your life.

Our physical bodies represent the earthly home for our souls. They are the outer shells that God uses as vessels to accomplish His will with on this earth. Our souls that reside inside of our bodies, during our life on earth, represent the essence of who we are as human beings connected to God. Our souls contain the inner senses of sight and hearing.

These senses are the spiritual vaults that God uses to securely deposit His divine instructions for our lives inside of us. They allow us to perceive things in the spiritual realm. Their application grants us the strength to generate the power from within our human bodies to heal from our hurts. They also represent the tools that we are able to employ in order to summon the power from inside of ourselves to accomplish things that seem to be impossible to our physical perception.

Our success in life is birthed inside of ourselves in the spiritual realm before it manifests itself in the physical realm of our lives. In order to activate what God deposits in us we must engage in the practices of prayer and meditation. These practices allow us to properly align our souls with the source energy of The Great I AM. They equip us with the ability to see ourselves and others from the perspective of the Great I AM.

Light vs Darkness

The will of the adversary is done when we make decisions that cause us to drift away from God's light. The adversary deals in the details of distractions. Distractions are the elements that lead to broken mental focus, which eventually manifests itself into broken dreams. No matter how far you may drift away from His light, God never leaves the throne of grace. This life is a journey of obedience to reflect God's will and not a journey to match His perfection. God knows the frailty of our humanity. He is our creator and the source of all light.

The Apostle Paul speaks of his own imperfection as a human being in the book of Romans. In chapter 7 verses

21-25 he states, "I find then a law, that evil is present with me, the one who wills to do good. For I delight in the law of God according to the inward man. But I see another law in my members, warring against the law of my mind, and bringing me into captivity to the law of sin which is in my members. O wretched man that I am! Who will deliver me from this body of death? I thank God through Jesus Christ our Lord!"

The Apostle Paul knew of his frailty as a human being but he also knew what it took to regain his sense of focus pertaining to doing the will of God above the desires of his human flesh. If you are reading this and have lost your focus, just know that prayer is the first step needed to bring you back home to the light of God. The power of I AM is always with you.

If you ever take a road trip you may rely upon a GPS system to navigate your trip. Modern navigation systems feature turn by turn directions that guide you to your destination. There is also a feature in them that will reroute you when you make a turn that is contrary to the original route that the GPS directed you toward. If you trust the GPS system, it will guide you with turn by turn instructions to the right place, as long as it is a place that can be located on a map.

The Spirit of God is the GPS system for our lives. On the road of life, our destinations are given to us by God. The Holy Spirit is the heaven sent agent that guides us to the destination that God has for us. Even when we may take a turn in life that may be contrary to the will of God, the Holy Spirit is always there to assist us in rerouting us toward God's original destination for our lives.

The Holy Spirit is in place to keep us focused and control any potential distractions that vie to place our lives off course. In his letter to the church at Ephesus the Apostle Paul expounds upon this concept. He states, "For you were once darkness, but now you are light in the Lord. Walk as children of light (for the Spirit is in all goodness, righteousness, and truth), finding out what is acceptable to the Lord" (Ephesians 5:8-10).

In life, the decisions that we make are the ultimate reflections of who we believe we are and what we believe we deserve. Our daily news gives us constant reminders of the activities of darkness. The darkness that we see in our world is spiritual in nature and often manifested physically in the form of senseless violence.

The most dangerous weapon in this world is a person who lacks a sense of divine purpose in their life and simultaneously has a heart filled with the dark entities of anger and hatred. A person in this state feels that their life does not have value and neither does anyone else's. As believers in God our lives are not immune to the realities of the darkness in our world. We do however have irrevocable access to our daily bread in the form of God's word. This word brings to us constant reminders of the proclivities of God's light.

The most powerful weapon in this world is a person who has a sense of their life's purpose and simultaneously has a heart filled with the light entities of love and kindness. A person in this state knows that their life has value and they can clearly see the value that everyone else's life has as well. The light that we see in our world is spiritual in nature and is often manifested physically in the form of unconditional love. It is through love that we best reflect the light of God.

In the book of 1st John chapter 4 verses 12-13 it states, "No one has seen God at any time. If we love one another, God abides in us, and His love has been perfected in us. By this we know that we abide in Him, and He in us, because He has given us of His spirit."

The Power of I AM

The book of Exodus records of God speaking to Moses at a burning bush on Mt. Nebo (Exodus 3:2-6). In our modern times, I have heard from God in a dream or in a still small voice within my heart. Your experience hearing from Him may be similar to mine. As I mentioned earlier, God's instructions to us come from the Holy Spirit whose presence was sent to earth to mentor God's children after Jesus ascended into heaven.

The Holy Spirit provides answers to us directly from heaven. His answers are confirmed through our feelings of inner peace when we make decisions. He was sent here to guide us to success while we inhabit the earth. He is found inside of our hearts and He is clearly heard when we learn to decrease the volume of our ego. He represents the I AM power that connects each of us to God.

The Holy Spirit is the divine power mechanism that makes the object of your faith truly come alive. His mentorship provides the detailed plans that will ultimately transform your seed of faith into a fulfilled promise of God over time. He can guide us to a successful future but He resides in the moment of now.

"In the book of Romans chapter 8 verses it states, "For as many as are led by the Spirit of God, these are sons of God. For you did not receive the spirit of bondage again to fear, but you received the Spirit of adoption by whom we cry out, 'Abba, Father.' The Spirit Himself bears witness with our spirit that we are children of God, and if children, the heirs of God and joint heirs with Christ, if indeed we suffer with Him, that we may also be glorified together." (Romans 8:14-17). In this passage of scripture, the Apostle Paul was artfully explaining the relationship between God's children and the Holy Spirit. The power of the Holy Spirit ultimately unifies us with God.

The Signs of I AM

When the I AM power of God is alive and working within a person, there are several characteristics that the individual will display. The Apostle Paul lists them as fruits of the spirit in the book of Galatians. He states, "But the fruit of the Spirit is love, joy, peace, longsuffering, kindness, goodness, faithfulness, gentleness, self-control. Against such there is no law. And those who are Christ's have crucified the flesh with its passions and desires. If we live in the Spirit, let us also walk in the Spirit." (Galatians 5:22-25). Each fruit of the Spirit represents a divine branch that extends from the tree of God consciousness.

If the power of God lives inside of you it is impossible for the world not to see it. The world may not understand what it sees but it cannot deny the signs of I AM. In his first letter to the church at Corinth the Apostle Paul writes, "These things we also speak, not in words which man's wisdom teaches but which the Holy Spirit teaches, comparing spiritual things with spiritual. But the natural man does not receive the things of the Spirit of God, for they are foolishness to him; nor can he know them, because they are spiritually discerned" (1 Corinthians 2:13-14).

The I AM power will compel you to do good things on this earth. It will never lead you to harm others or engage in activities that bring dishonor to God. It is prayer that keeps the I AM power strong inside of you. It is important to have faith and it is important to exercise your faith. Your faith in action is a display of the I AM power at work. In the book of James chapter 2 verses 16-17 it states, "Thus also faith by itself, if it does not have works, is dead. But someone will say, you have faith and I have works. Show me your faith without your works, and I will show you my faith by my works."

The activation of the Holy Spirit will equip you with the wisdom, knowledge and understanding that will allow you to excel in any area of your life. Your success as a child of God is connected to your ability to be obedient to the instructions of the Holy Spirit. Jesus spoke about this in chapter 16 of the gospel of John stating, "I still have many things to say to you, but you cannot bear them now. However, when He, the Spirit of truth, has come, He will guide you into all truth; for He will not speak on His own authority, but whatever He hears He will speak; and He will tell you things to come. He will glorify Me, for He will take of what is Mine and declare it to you" (John 16: 12-15).

Listen to what the Holy Spirit speaks to you and you will undoubtedly achieve the destiny that God has designed for your life. In order to clearly hear His instructions, you must play your trump card of faith. With it you will find success in both Americas and you will reflect the omnipotent power of God each day that you live. It is my prayer that God will continue to bless your life and that you will choose to bless the lives of others.

Chapter 14 Questions

1. Do I feel the power of I AM alive inside of me?
   _____
   _____
   _____
   _____
   _____

2. Do I feel that I am currently walking in God's light?
   _____
   _____
   _____
   _____
   _____

3. Do I know how to get back home to God's light if I have drifted away from it?
   _____
   _____
   _____
   _____

PART THREE

THE PROMISED LAND

Chapter 15

Promised Land Faith

There will be times in life when you may feel that the dream that God has placed inside of you seems to be impossible to accomplish. If you have faith, the method of how you will accomplish it will be revealed over time. The transition from something first being believed for until it is actually accomplished often involves a series of steps. Dr. Martin Luther King Jr. once said, "Faith is taking the first step even when you don't see the whole staircase." If you believe in God you must believe that with His help there is nothing good on this earth that cannot be accomplished. In order for your faith to work you must know that God wants the best for your life.

It is imperative that you also know that God desires to see you living a blessed and prosperous life. Since people did not create you, you must refrain from allowing their negative opinions to discourage you from believing in the promises that God reveals to you. In life, we often look to our peers for guidance in certain situations. It is important to remember that even though their opinions may come from a place of love, it may not match what God has revealed to you.

You cannot let the fear that someone else may attempt to impose upon you cause your faith to waver. As a believer in God, your faith is rooted in His promises and not in the opinions of others. Following the opinions of others can sometimes lead to heartache and place you off the pathway of God's will for your life. We order our blessings from the menu of heaven through our faith. In the opposite manner, we order our curses from the menu of hell through our fears. It is human nature to feel fear but it is by divine order that we employ the power of faith to overcome it.

Faithfulness and Fearfulness

In the book of Numbers, the benefits of faithfulness and the price of fearfulness are illuminated in the story of twelve spies that God's servant Moses sent to view the Promised Land of Canaan. And the Lord spoke to Moses, saying, "Send men to spy out the land of Canaan, which I am giving to the children of Israel; from each tribe of their fathers you shall send a man, every one a leader among them" (Numbers 13:2). Moses in obedience to God's command sent twelve men each representing the twelve sons of Jacob.

The land of Canaan was the land that God promised to give to Jacob and his descendants (Genesis 28:13). God was giving them entry back into the Promised Land of Canaan nearly 400 years after Jacob and his sons fled the famine that ushered Joseph into power. God called upon

Moses to lead them out of slavery and into the place that He prepared for them to inhabit.

After a period of forty days, in which they dedicated to spying out the land of Canaan, the spies brought back a detailed report of what they saw. "Then they told him, and said: We went to the land where you sent us. It truly flows with milk and honey, and this is its fruit. Nevertheless, the people who dwell in the land are strong; the cities are fortified and very large; moreover, we saw the descendants of Anak there" (Numbers 13:27-28). After ten of the spies gave the aforementioned negative report to Moses, one of the spies named Caleb challenged their fearful assertions with the spirit of faith. Then Caleb quieted the people before Moses, and said, "Let us go up at once and take possession, for we are well able to overcome it" (Numbers 13:30).

The ten spies held onto their fears and did not share the vision of faith that Caleb possessed. But the men who had gone up with him said, "We are not able to go up against the people, for they are stronger than we." And they gave the children of Israel a bad report of the land which they had spied out, saying, "The land through which we have gone as spies is a land that devours its inhabitants, and all the people whom we saw in it are men of great stature. There we saw the giants; and we were like grasshoppers in our own sight, and so we were in their sight" (Numbers 13:31-33).

The words of the ten spies caused fear to set in upon the children of Israel. They began to complain against Moses, speak glowingly of death, and entertain thoughts of replacing Moses with a new leader who they hoped would lead them back to Egypt, the place of their enslavement. In their choosing fear over faith, they showed open contempt for the will of God and a tremendous lack of faith in the truthfulness of His promise to lead them safely into the land that He promised to them.

Joshua stood in faith along with Caleb by saying: "The land we passed through to spy out is an exceedingly good land. If the Lord delights in us, He will bring us into this land and give it to us, a land which flows with milk and honey. Only do not rebel against the Lord, nor fear the people of the land, for they are our bread; their protection has departed from them, and the Lord is with us. Do not fear them" (Numbers 14: 7-9).

Instead of finding inspiration in the words that Joshua and Caleb spoke to them, the children of Israel began to grab stones to kill them with. This turn of events compelled God to make His presence known. He immediately spoke to Moses and stated "How long will these people reject Me? And how long will they not believe Me, with all the signs which I have performed among them? I will strike them with the pestilence and disinherit them, and I will make you a nation greater and mightier than they" (Numbers 14:11-12).

Moses did not agree with God's assessment and sought to reason with Him on behalf of the children of Israel. In verses 15 and 16 of Numbers chapter 14 he states, "Now if You kill these people as one man, then the nations which have heard of Your fame will speak, saying, Because the Lord was not able to bring this people to the land which He swore to give them, therefore He killed them in the wilderness." "Pardon the iniquity of this people, I pray, according to the greatness of Your mercy, just as You have forgiven this people, from Egypt even until now" (Numbers 14:19).

In response to the plea of Moses, God decided to show mercy on the children of Israel. He then gave Moses clear instructions of His plans to punish the children of Israel in direct response to their unbelief in His promise to them. He said to Moses, "Say to them, As I live, says the Lord, just as you have spoken in My hearing, so I will do to you: The carcasses of you who have complained against

Me shall fall in this wilderness, all of you who were numbered, according to your entire number, from twenty years old and above.

Except for Caleb the son of Jephunneh and Joshua the son of Nun, you shall by no means enter the land which I swore I would make you dwell in. But your little ones, whom you said would be victims, I will bring in, and they know the land which you have despised. But as for you, your carcasses shall fall in this wilderness. And your sons shall be shepherds in the wilderness forty years, and bear the brunt of your infidelity, until your carcasses are consumed in the wilderness. According to the number of the days in which you spied out the land, forty days, for each day you shall bear your guilt one year, namely forty years, and you shall know my rejection" (Numbers 14:28-34).

The Faith of Joshua

God was true to His word, and after forty years of wandering in the wilderness as a result of the fearful report of ten of the twelve spies, the children of Israel were finally camped outside of the Promised Land of Canaan once again. They were led there by Joshua who became their new leader after Moses died during their forty years of wandering in the wilderness.

In chapter 1 of the book of Joshua, God gives instructions to Joshua following the death of Moses. In verse 2 of chapter 1 on He states, "Moses My Servant is dead. Now therefore, arise, go over this Jordan, you and all this people, to the land which I am giving to them the children of Israel." He went on to state to Joshua, "No man shall be able to stand before you all the days of your life; as I was with Moses, so I will be with you. I will not leave you nor forsake you. Be strong and of good courage, for to his people you shall divide as an inheritance the land which I swore to their fathers to give them" (Joshua 1:5-6).

Equipped with the power of God, Joshua chose to send two men to spy in the Promised Land of Canaan and to bring him back a report of what they saw. It is fitting that Joshua knew to only send two spies as opposed to twelve, which is the number that Moses sent to spy out the land forty years prior. Joshua was one of the two men who brought back a faith filled report for Moses and now forty years later, he knew that all he needed was two men of faith to spy for him. "So the two men returned, descended from the mountain, and crossed over; and they came to Joshua the son of Nun, and told him all that had befallen them." And they said to Joshua, "Truly the Lord has delivered all the land into our hands, for indeed all the inhabitants of the country are fainthearted because of us" (Joshua 2:23-24).

Who Is Our Joshua

If I take a bottle of water and remove the cap from it, the contents of my bottle would be left exposed to the elements. The precious contents of the bottle would also be at risk for spilling outside of the bottle. I would find myself in a situation hoping that the bottle as it was constructed would be tall enough to secure the contents inside of it. The bottle itself was designed as a home for my contents, a place where they are supposed to be nurtured. It was not designed to secure the contents from the elements or to keep the contents from spilling outside of the bottle. The responsibility of protecting the contents and securing them is that of the bottle cap.

In the black community today, our figurative bottles are represented in the form of black women, our contents are black children, and our bottle caps are represented by the lives of black men. In order for black Americans to reach our Promised Land, black men must secure our journey there.

As of December 31, 2015, there were approximately 501,300 black men incarcerated in the United States of America. Each of these incarcerated men represent missing vessels in a teetering community that desperately needs their contributions. There is a hole in the life of someone living on the outside of prison walls due to their absence. Just imagine for a moment if all of these men were free and earning an honest living in our society. If these men earned an average of 30,000 per year, after taxes, that would represent approximately fifteen billion dollars that would greatly impact the economic landscape of black Americans annually.

If these men were responsible God fearing men, they could be potential role models in their own families and for the young people that would encounter them. I understand that real life is much more complex than a Sociological equation, but the aforementioned dollar figure provides for us a glimpse of what the future of the black community can potentially reflect when we are freed from the wiles of the criminal justice system.

I was raised by an incredible black woman, but it was impossible for her to teach me how to be a man. Black women are undoubtedly intelligent, they are beautiful and they are strong. With all of the wonderful attributes that they possess, it is still not their responsibility to represent both the figurative bottles and caps for our community. There is currently a generation of black males who have grown up living without the guidance of strong black male leadership. These individuals have grown up uncertain of the core concepts of what the true measures of manhood represent. I grew up without my father present in my life. I was blessed to have my grandfather and uncles in my life to protect the contents of my destiny. They were there to educate me on the principles of manhood.

From them, I learned core concepts such as: making my word my bond, and ensuring that the people and things that I was responsible for were taken care of. They taught me to value education and to develop self-discipline. They explained to me the virtues of high character and displayed for me the benefits of high integrity. They informed me about the importance of daily prayer in the facilitation of a successful life. They taught me that being committed to one woman and modeling the reflection of God's love with her was more rewarding than being a player seeking to feed the appetite of my ego. The most important thing that they taught me was to be a man of faith.

Just as my grandfather and uncles protected the contents of my destiny, I have sought to do the same thing for others in my family and community. There are some people reading this book that did not grow up with positive role models with traits similar to the individuals that I was blessed with. Through the words in this book, it is my desire to share with others the seeds of black American prosperity that have been harvested in my life from the influence of my grandfather and uncles.

The greatest threat to the system of white supremacy is the critically thinking, self-educated and self-disciplined black male. The aforementioned system rests well when it has black males under correctional control or when they are basking in the sunlight of effeminacy. Today, I encourage each black male reading these words to protect the contents of the bottles in your area of influence. You are most powerful when you are present. Our Joshua is currently alive within your midst.

For black Americans in the United States, our Moses was represented in form of Dr. Martin Luther King Jr., and his brother Aaron was represented in the form of Malcolm X. Dr. King embodied our collective spirit while Malcolm X represented our collective strength. Both of their lives were snuffed out by those within the estuaries of power before they could lead black Americans into the Promised Land of economic equality and social equity.

The work of Dr. King and Malcolm X produced Civil Rights legislation but it was unable to produce the level of economic and political power that black Americans need in order to help level the socio-economic and socio-political playing fields in this country. Since 1968, there have been several men to step forward and attempt to lead black Americans into the Promised Land. I am pretty sure that you know some of their names. They have accomplished noted achievements but none of them has been able to lead black Americans into the Promised Land.

A great number of observers felt in 2008, that President Obama represented the Joshua like figure that would lead black Americans into the figurative Promised Land that Dr. Martin Luther King and Malcolm X spoke about in the 1960's. President Obama's term in the White House showed that he is a good statesman who is more of an inspirational figure than a revolutionary leader. He is not responsible for the collective success of black Americans.

The collective success of black Americans is not the sole responsibility of any God created individual. It is not the responsibility of an elected official, admired athlete or celebrated entertainer. The collective success of black-Americans is found within the principle of faith. Black Americans must believe that we are well able and deserve to possess the Promised Land of economic and political power.

For so many years black Americans have believed the incorrect report that European domination has given to us. For generations, we have internalized the falsehoods that we are second class citizens, that we are anthropologically subordinate, that we are only deemed capable of achieving greatness in entertainment and athletics and that we cannot rely upon the collective group to support the dreams of individual members. Since the inceptive founding of this nation, black Americans have lived our lives under the lie drenched cloak of being undervalued, underestimated and marginalized. The report that we believe must change in order for us to reach our Promised Land.

In his *I've Been to the Mountaintop* speech at Mason Temple, the night before his death, Dr. King spoke of seeing the Promised Land. He stated, "I just want to do God's will. And He's allowed me to go up to the mountain. And I've looked over and I've seen the Promised Land. I may not get there with you. But I want you to know tonight that we, as a people, will get to the Promised Land."

It has been fifty years since our Moses physically departed from this world. In his absence, black Americans have continued to fight through the wilderness of economic inequality and social inequity. I believe that we are the people that Dr. King saw in his vision. He spied out the Promised Land for us and brought back a report of faith to us. We are the Joshua generation that will inhabit the Promised Land. Our faith will unlock the key to God's will for us and our unity will clear the pathway to our success. I do not believe that there is one individual who will be the Joshua for black Americans in our modern time. I believe that our Joshua is represented in a God inspired spirit and not a God created individual.

To make it into the Promised Land, it will take a collective spirit that chooses to believe the report of faith before we can earn the rewards of it. Black Americans have always had what it takes to possess the Promised Land. We have unfortunately spent the last 400 years believing the wrong report about who we are. This is in our hands to change. God has led us to the edge of the wilderness but we must possess the faith to leave it behind for the land that we are well able to possess.

The book of Joshua records the Israelites finally inhabiting the land that God originally promised to their patriarch Abraham. It states, "So the Lord gave to Israel all the land of which He had sworn to give to their fathers, and they took possession of it and dwelt in it. The Lord gave them rest all around, according to all that He had sworn to their fathers. And not a man of all their enemies stood against them; the Lord delivered all their enemies into their hand. Not a word failed of any good thing which the Lord had spoken to the house of Israel. All came to pass" (Joshua 21:43-45).

After nearly 400 years of living in this land, I believe that the Promised Land of economic equality and social equity is at hand for African Americans. Our success is the reward for the survival of our ancestors. Through all the atrocities and injustices that they faced, they never stopped moving forward in faith. Just as the Israelites did, I believe that African Americans will take possession of what God promised to our ancestors. With the power of God's spirit, they built this country piece by piece. With the power of that same spirit, we will finally make America great for the first time, person by person. This will be accomplished regardless of whether or not mainstream America chooses to support our efforts.

The election of Donald Trump to the presidency is the sign for us to leave fear behind and trust in the power of our collective unity. Donald Trump is a man who sits in a powerful earthly position. He is a human being just as each of us is. The God that we serve is more powerful than any man.

For the sake of this country, I hope that Donald Trump does a good job as the President of the United States, just as I hoped his predecessors would when they were in office. My hope for him to succeed does not expunge the fact that he has used rhetoric that has promoted racial discrimination and insensitivity to several groups that are classified as minorities. He represents a modern-day Pharaoh sitting on the throne of social and institutional oppression. Just as the Pharaoh did in the book of Exodus, he ultimately has no choice but to let God's people go.

The actions of the man currently living in The White House are of lesser importance than the solutions for prosperity that we as African Americans must decide to implement in our own homes. None of us living today has the ability to know what the next several years will bring, but our confidence is shaped by our belief in our God who holds our future in the palm of His hand. I encourage you to be prayerful, I desire for you to stay blessed, and most of all, I implore you to keep your faith strong. May God bless you and keep you and may heaven have a smile upon you.

Chapter 15 Questions

1. What has God promised to me?
   _____
   _____
   _____
   _____

2. Do I believe that God will keep His word to me?
   _____
   _____
   _____
   _____

3. Do I believe that I am ready to enter into the Promised Land?
   _____
   _____
   _____

Conclusion

Faith is the ultimate trump card that will create success for anyone who applies it. In this book, I have described examples of people who have used faith to overcome circumstances that seemed to be impossible to accomplish. The principles of faith are the required prerequisites that God's children need in order to succeed no matter who the President of The United States is. I am not afraid of Donald Trump and you should not fear him either. I am not afraid of the Republican Party or the Democratic Party either. My faith in God does not permit me to fear them. You should not fear them as well. I am also proud to be a child of God, and I am also equally as proud to be an American of African descent.

    I will be the first person to admit that I am no better than anyone else on this earth. I am a human being who tries to represent God's light each day that I live. My life is an example of God using an obedient servant to do His will on this earth. I wrote this book with the intention to inspire anyone who reads it in applying the principles of faith to reach their goals. Even though this particular book was targeted towards black Americans, the presented concepts and shared principles are God inspired recipes for dream achievement that anyone can apply to their life.

    I wish I lived in a world in which the color of my skin did not matter. I wish the United States of America was truly one nation under God with liberty and justice for all.

That is not the case as of today, but with our efforts things will continually improve for us on this earth.

I am blessed every day to be able to use my God given gifts to inspire those who see my work. My success is due to each of you who support my efforts in seeking to make this world a much better place than I was born into. I am grateful for each of you that took your time to read the words that God inspired me to share with you. I know that some people who read my books may never read a Bible or attend a church service. I am honored that God saw fit to use my life to touch yours.

My assignment in this world is to elevate the way people think about themselves. This will empower them to elevate their communities. Those in the communities will then be inspired to elevate the nation which will in turn uplift the world and bring it closer to the face of God. It is my sincere prayer that my words touch your heart and through them you are able to clearly see the perfect image of God's love for you. Please allow these words to permeate your spirit and inspire you to live out the purpose that God has assigned for your life. I thank you for your time, and I pray that the blessings of God will overtake your life.

BIBLIOGRAPHY

Chapter 1

Genesis 15:13-14 NKJV

Chapter 2

"Where Do We Go From Here?" Copyright 2018 The Heirs to the Estate of Martin Luther King, Jr.

Luhby, T. (2015, February 27). Asian Americans are quickly catching whites in the wealth race. *CNN*. Retrieved from http://money.cnn.com/2015/02/26/news/economy/asians-wealth-whites/index.html.

Woodson, C. (1933). *The Mis-Education Of The Negro*. (pp. xiii). Washington, DC: The Associated Publishers, Inc.

Chapter 3

Joshua 1: 8-9 NKJV

Chapter 4

American History. (2011). Paragon Books Ltd. Bath, UK.

Carson, E.A. & Anderson, A. (2016). Prisoners in 2015. *Bureau of Justice Statistics*. 6-13. Retrieved from http://www.bjs.gov/index.cfm?ty=pbdetail&iid=5869

History.comStaff. (2011). Compromise of 1877. A+E Networks. New York, NY. Retrieved from http://www.history.com/topics/us-presidents/compromise-of-1877

Primary Documents in American History. Morril Act. *Library of Congress*. Retrieved from https://www.loc.gov/rr/program/bib/ourdocs/Morrill.html

Short, D. (2017). The Illinois Department of Corrections Fiscal Year 2016 Annual Report. *Illinois Department of Corrections*.74-75. Retrieved from https://www.illinois.gov/idoc/reportsandstatistics/Pages/AnnualReports.aspx.

Proverbs 1:7 NKJV
Proverbs 2:6 NKJV
Joshua 3:5 NKJV

Chapter 5

Taylor, Q. (2009). *America I am Black Facts*. Smiley Books. New York, NY.

"Jomo Kenyatta on the Arrival of Christianity" is reconstructed from various anecdotal accounts.

Genesis 1:26-27 NKJV
Genesis 9:20-27 NKJV
John 1:1-3 NKJV
John 1:14 NKJV
Revelation 1:14-15 NKJV

Chapter 6

Forbes The Riches People in America Special Issue. (2017, October). Forbes Magazine, 198(5), 124-125.

Rand, A. (1957). *Atlas Shrugged*. Random House. New York, NY.

Ritzer, G. (2000). *Classical Sociological Theory*. McGraw-Hill. New York, NY.

"Where Do We Go From Here?" Copyright 2018 The Heirs to the Estate of Martin Luther King, Jr.

Mark 10:45 NKJV

Chapter 7

Jeremiah 1:5 NKJV
Jeremiah 29:11 NKJV
John 14:15-17 NKJV
John 17:14-18 NKJV
Philippians 4:19 NKJV
www.megamillions.com
www.powerball.com

Chapter 8

I Samuel 16:7 NKJV
Matthew 14:28-31 NKJV
Romans 12:2 NKJV
II Timothy 1:7 NKJV
Hebrews 11:1 NKJV

Chapter 9

Mark 5:23 NKJV
Mark 5:35 NKJV
Mark 5:39 NKJV
John 16:7 NKJV
John 16:12-14 NKJV

Chapter 10

Joshua 14:7 NKJV
Psalms 46:10 NKJV
Habakkuk 2:2-3 NKJV
Mark 11:24 NKJV
Romans 4:16-17 NKJV
"Chinese Bamboo Tree" is reconstructed from various anecdotal accounts.

Chapter 11

Genesis 28:12-13 NKJV
Genesis 28:15 NKJV
Genesis 32:26 NKJV
Lamentations 3:22-23 NKJV
Hebrews 11:6 NKJV
Hebrews 13:8 NKJV

Chapter 12

Genesis 5:5-8 NKJV
Genesis 37:21-36 NKJV
Genesis 39:23 NKJV
Genesis 41:12 NKJV
Genesis 41:16 NKJV
Genesis 41:40 NKJV
Proverbs 18:16 NKJV
Matthew 25:21 NKJV

Chapter 13

I Kings 17:9-16 NKJV
Psalms 46:10 NKJV
Matthew 21:19 NKJV

Matthew 21:21 NKJV
Romans 14:13 NKJV
I Corinthians 6:19-20 NKJV

Chapter 14

Exodus 2:14 NKJV
Exodus 3:2-6 NKJV
Exodus 3:12 NKJV
John 8:53-58 NKJV
John 16:12-15 NKJV
Romans 7:21-25 NKJV
Romans 8:14-17 NKJV
I Corinthians 2:13-14 NKJV
Ephesians 5:8-10 NKJV
Galatians 5:22-25 NKJV
James 2:16-17 NKJV
I John 4:12-13 NKJV

Chapter 15

Brainy Quote.com, "Martin Luther King, Jr. Quotes," https://www.brainyquote.com/quotes/authors/m/martin_luther_king_jr.html.

"I've Been to The Mountaintop," Copyright 2018 The Heirs to the Estate of Martin Luther King, Jr.

Carson, E.A. & Anderson, A. (2016). Prisoners in 2015. *Bureau of Justice Statistics*. 13-15. Retrieved from http://www.bjs.gov/index.cfm?ty=pbdetail&iid=5869

"May God bless you and keep you" is reconstructed from the author's childhood interactions with Elder Willie B. Jackson.

Genesis 28:13 NKJV
Joshua 1:5-6 NKJV
Joshua 2:23-24 NKJV
Numbers 13:27-28 NKJV
Numbers 13:30-33 NKJV
Numbers 14:7-9 NKJV
Numbers 14: 11-12 NKJV
Numbers 14: 15-16 NKJV
Numbers 14:19 NKJV
Numbers 14:28-34 NKJV

ABOUT THE AUTHOR

Eric Moore is the author of the book titled Playing The Trump Card: Using Faith to Succeed in Two Americas. This is his second book. His first book titled Living For Friday Dreading Sunday Night was published in 2012. He is originally from Detroit, Michigan but he currently resides in Philadelphia, Pennsylvania. He is a life coach, motivational speaker and a I/O Psychologist. He specializes in encouraging others to discover their life purpose and he seeks to inspire them to strive for lives of excellence. He is a man who speaks truth to power and works tirelessly to empower the minds of those that feel powerless. If you desire to book him for speaking engagements or to discuss the contents of this book please send all inquiries to emoorespeaks@gmail.com.

Made in the USA
Middletown, DE
18 November 2023

43029570R00102